WANDERINGS
IN LAKELAND

VETERAN SHEPHERD OF WESTMORLAND FELLS CARRYING A STRAY
SHEEP ON HIS SHOULDERS

WANDERINGS IN LAKELAND

by

William T. Palmer, F.R.G.S., M.B.O.U., F.S.A. Scot.

With Fifteen Illustrations
by
JOHN HARDMAN

SKEFFINGTON & SON, LTD.

47 Princes Gate - - - - - - - *S.W.7*

LONDON : NEW YORK : MELBOURNE : SYDNEY : CAPE TOWN

THIS BOOK IS PRODUCED IN
COMPLETE CONFORMITY WITH THE
AUTHORIZED ECONOMY STANDARDS

59.571

First Edition,   October, 1945
Second Edition,   July, 1946
Third Edition, December, 1946

PRINTED IN
GREAT BRITAIN
BY THE ANCHOR
PRESS, LIMITED,
TIPTREE, ESSEX

PREFACE

For the first forty years of my life I lived in Lakeland; I was schooled there and climbed big trees; later, I wandered about the fells and dales, lakes and rivers and moors, and studied the folks—farmers, shepherds, coachmen, guards, ostlers, huntsmen, anglers and poacher folk. The strong and variegated characters of these are shown in my pages—to a great extent their lives were mine, their play was mine. I went out fox-hunting, and also did some rock-climbing, which (according to modern standards) was meagre and not important; but left me with the joy of great rock spires, mighty rock buttresses, deep clifts, narrow ledges and the wonderful display of light and shade and weather in highest Cumbria.

In *Wanderings in Lakeland* I have turned many pages of memories, recorded many pictures and stories of roads and coach-craft, showing life as it was and is. Except that the rocks are more frequented and the paths well beaten, there is little change on the highest moors and mountains.

In the years I discovered other Lakeland watersides than my own, their villages and anglers. As to cycling, I tried to learn on an old boneshaker built by some wheelwright; trips usually finished in hedge or ditch. The first pedal-cyclist on our road was a marvel and a show. Later I took the fraternity rightly as "the salt of the earth".

What life will be in the future is beyond my knowledge. I have seen great expanses, even entire watersheds, taken into municipal and national ownership. I therefore ask the reader to accept this book as a compilation of pages, notes and sketches written over many years, and now revised and put into a permanent book.

WILLIAM T. PALMER.

CONTENTS

ILLUSTRATIONS
by John Hardman

9

CHAPTER ONE

WHEN HORSED COACHES CROSSED LAKELAND

The Road to Keswick—"Coachee"—The Yard of Tin—The Christmas Mail

FIFTY-odd years ago, as a lad, I tramped the old coach-road across the Lake District, from Windermere station through Ambleside, Rydal, Grasmere, Dunmail Raise, and Wythburn to Keswick. As I walked, the horsed mails with their red-coated coachmen used to trot past, and a fine memory they give. The horses were good and clever; there was polish on harness and on swingletrees, and never being covetous in the matter of travel, I rejoiced. The old horn was blown as the coach neared cross-roads and hamlets, and at the signal some person would come out for letters which were thrown out, without the slackening of the horses.

I wonder if I can recall every mile of the old road, and its tricks. Hurrying motor-buses, charas and private cars have caused many changes: the crossing of the Lake District is no longer a good half-day's journey, with a meal at Grasmere or Wythburn, but a mere incident in a morning's run. The road-side has changed almost out of recognition as well. The villages have extended on both ends, and there are many houses in places where formerly the bracken and heather grew or where the pasture was covered with golden buttercups. If you knew the old road, of course you will follow my story all the easier, but the Lake District coach-road is historic, and more people know it by reading than have set eyes or feet upon it at any time.

I suppose Windermere station has not mightily changed in my lifetime. The former little rubbish-tip to the left of the white gates has been smoothed into a tiny and welcome park at the expense of the local authority. The company could have done the job fifty years ago and benefited their waiting passengers at trifling expense.

Rigg's Hotel still looks down from its terrace on to the station front and gates: to me it has always been an aloof place, where strangers seemed welcome and "locals" not encouraged. I may be wrong about this. The foreground of the hotel has been altered: a big border of rhododendrons and laurels has been dug away in order to provide a "lay-by" for motor-buses passing between Kendal and Keswick. Only a few of these enter the station yard to meet the trains.

I have tried hard to remember an earlier fountain than this at the cross-roads outside the railway station. In my young days there was rarely water in it, except on cold days in winter. In summer the tap was turned in vain—and one made inward comments about the influences which compelled wanderers to drink in hotel or refreshment-room. In those days cafés of the ordinary type were unknown, and few shops and cottages in Windermere provided food and drink. 'Twas said, with wickedness, that plutocratic Windermere disliked the railway excursionists, the thirsty ramblers. Even the cyclist was not welcomed, and I believe that the C.T.C. had quite a scrimmage before the needs of its members were properly catered for. The winged wheel, however, is now as constant as the A.A. and R.A.C. signs.

The cluster of houses at the head of High Street, just outside the railway station, has apparently changed but little in the years : there is the same bank at the corner, though its cognomen has changed, but the printing-works on the Ambleside road no longer turn out a weekly newspaper. Forty years ago there were two weeklies at Ambleside as well as this Windermere issue, but nowadays the whole Lake District gets its news from Kendal (one paper where there were three) and Penrith (two instead of three). Some day perhaps I shall ponder on the effect of losing these amusing little papers, some of which existed for "Parish Pump" politics, but also gave local notes which will be the basis of history in times to come. Forty years hence, the files of these lost weeklies will be searched for items which have become important and interesting, news which otherwise has not been recorded at all.

Opposite the old printing-office in my first tramps was a recess with three ends : on the right a steep rugged path went past a cottage for Orrest Head, one of the world's finest look-outs. The route was almost concealed, and half-way up there was a scramble round an intrusive bit of property owned by someone who did not love public access. The middle gate was definitely private ; and I do not recollect that there was any obvious sign on the next, which was the lower path to Troutbeck and is now the easiest access to Orrest Head.

My early memories of that path are not cheerful : the hedges came very close, the mud was sticky, and garden rubbish was shot into it almost knee-deep at places. There was no findable cross-access from the Troutbeck path to Orrest Head, though I believe there was always a public right of way. Nowadays, of course, the paths are wide, pleasant, and easily graded.

To return to the main road : Elleray, once the home of Professor John Wilson ("Christopher North"), is now a girls' school, and some big residences on the hillsides have been demolished, and their grounds divided among several smaller houses. In my boyhood it was considered to be a mark of intimate knowledge to strike the path from the church down to Millerground with its ancient ferry to Wray and Hawkshead. There was no indication of the thoroughfare; the path was usually muddy and the brook a gardener's tip.

To Cook's House, the road-sides have changed but little, and the lofty garden wall all covered with ivy which masks the entrance to the Patterdale road is older than my memories.

At Cook's House four roads meet: that to Ambleside, our main route, is four times its old width at least, and I have seen acres scraped off the Calgarth woods and buried in road metal. To Bowness, the south road has been opened at its entrance, but half a mile away, on the brink of a hill, the route is still narrow for the traffic it has to carry in summer-time. The Troutbeck or Kirkstone road seems to keep to its old condition, but it is certainly wider, for a grass strip of former days has been added to it.

The structure known as Cook's House has been rebuilt and enlarged some three times within my time, and I think that once at any rate the building was brought forward some yards. The first Cook's House I recall was the sort of four-room cottage which was tenanted by some humble worker on road or farm. It has long had a different type of owner. It's none the worse for that, of course. The garden, however, is usually pretty. I like gardens which the owners delight to share with the world, leaving low walls so that travellers can be refreshed by the flowers provided by God. In other places along this road, both fifty years ago and today, high stone walls and dense fences annoy me. I know one thick hedge which is backed by a chestnut paling so that no eye can possibly peep on the lawn of a certain owner.

In my boyhood the Calgarth Woods were mostly coppice with a few standards. The coppice was felled at twenty-year intervals for the oak bark and charcoal. The old Hall, with its skulls built into a staircase window, was clean away from all other buildings and needed some finding. Nowadays the lake-side is lined with villas reached by a private road, and there are houses scattered closely in the remaining woods, also in the long pasture which I knew as the Park.

The person who "developed" the Calgarth Woods estate is accused of another annoying trick. Originally, beyond the coppice wood, there was a quarter-mile of clear vision to the lake and up to the fells, a wonderful picture indeed. To prevent the new houses in the level pasture from being overlooked, some trees were planted alongside the road—and for years the first clear vision of Coniston Old Man, Wetherlam, Bowfell and the Langdale Pikes was blotted out. Latterly, however, a foot-path has been cut inside the timber belt, and gives the old beauties to those who know when and where to turn.

On the right hand now is the first of twenty milestones. Beyond it, on my early walks, I could reach a little brook of cold water with my drinking-cup. The curved pipe at the brow a few yards beyond was not dependable in dry weather—the only time there was any question of thirst at short intervals on the route. Both these drinking-places are lost now, for the tarmac comes close up to the wall.

To Troutbeck Bridge, the left-hand side of the road is strange to old memories. The oaks, some of them at any rate, remain, but they are in the road, now beyond the wall. Strip after strip of ground has been turned into roadway in order to straighten out a big and awkward bend. On the right-hand side I used to bid good morning to the famous wrestling umpire, Tom Longmire, who usually stood on the doorstep of his Sun Hotel. The chapel on the brow was built before my time, but the access was by foot-path only until the men of the congregation set to work with pick and spade and made an approach drive wide enough for a carriage. At the foot of the slope, the cottages have been rearranged and refronted, and two which projected at an angle into the road have been removed. I remember the four-horse coaches jigging round the corner, for they needed a lot of room.

Troutbeck Bridge was last widened only a few years back, and from it to Lowwood Hotel, the road has had countless slices thrown in on one side or other, or both, all the way. I remember the path alongside Calgarth Hall because it had the most villainous gravel in the whole county, gravel which caused the tired person, hurrying for a train at Windermere, to slip and stumble badly.

Beyond the second Calgarth lodge I have a memory of undulations, and looking about last year found that the road had been lifted to a higher level. A bit of hill would be shaved off and cast into the hollow beyond. At the field gate beyond Calgarth Hall Woods, it is delightful still to find that the lake is flashing close by.

Beyond the second milestone used to be Gipsy Lane, where caravans and camp-fires, begging children, fortune-telling women and idle men used to resort. Now they are forbidden. I find the gipsy folk resorting to car-parks next to garages—not exactly to the pleasure of people who are taking in petrol and oil at the adjacent pumps.

Onward a few yards, a drive goes off, taking a path to the Troutbeck road, and on the opposite side is a tiny church of "temporary" materials. At one time this had a fair active attendance, but it does not seem to be greatly cared for today. Several large mansions with many servants supported it—and these houses are either empty or with skeleton staffs.

From the road there are tantalizing slants across the lake to the green woods of Claife, and over the tree-tops there are bits of Langdale Pikes.

In the next dip, a bit of untidy woodland has been displaced by a pretty house. Fifty years back the glade had a rough timber shed and a tumbledown cottage standing thirty yards back from the road, beyond a gate. I was interested in the gate, which was always the loneliest and darkest place between Windermere and Ambleside, because here, in Mr. R. H. Sherard's Lake Country story, *Jacob Niemand*, the bank clerk was struck down, stunned and robbed under circumstances which attracted suspicion to the stranger Niemand. Mr. Sherard claimed to be a grand-nephew of William Wordsworth, if I remember rightly, and was domiciled at Outgate in the Hawkshead district for some seasons.

At the next corner to the left a Christmas gale tumbled over the trees in the grounds of the big house; they were piled in all directions and it was a long time before the last sign of disaster was cut out. The next straight has been trebled in width, and is recognized as a general halting-place for cars. The view is magnificent: a short green field falls to the alders and hawthorns next the lake; there is a mile of gleaming water, and then the tower of ninety-year-old Wray Castle in its oak woods, waves of oak and larch and pine one beyond the other for eight miles, and then the lilac walls of Coniston Fells on the horizon. We used to see more steamers in the old days, for the service was kept up until the lake froze in January. We also saw white-sailed yachts, real big craft leaning in the wind, for every big house on this shore had two or three, and had enthusiasts able and willing to sail them for pleasure and in races too. Today there are fewer and smaller yachts on Windermere, and their owners seem to live near Bowness Bay. And in the boat-houses up here, there is more likely to be a petrol-launch than a yacht, while the outlook on cruising has entirely changed.

Langdale Chase, on the left, is now a private hotel; it was one of the last mansions of the old luxurious type to be built in the Lake Country. A local comment was that more money was devoted to the two-storeyed boat-house at the foot of the grounds than was spent in the seven-year building of Wray Castle. I am not in a position to judge. The Chase woods are all built over.

The steep incline to Lowwood gives a fine view of Langdale Pikes, and of the lake which is here at its widest. The road from Troutbeck which comes in on the right beyond Langdale Chase is little used as a through route because it is steep and twisty. Not far up it is "Starve-crow Farm", where Stanley Weyman sited his novel. The inn at Lowwood and various local characters, pleasant and evil, are brought into the story, which deals with the early Chartist period. The old jail at Kendal, and the depraved magistrate-parson of Ambleside, are part of the tale.

The first Kendal and Windermere railway should have reached the lake shore at Lowwood, but Wordsworth led a fierce attack on the scheme, and the proposers had to halt at Birthwaite, near Orrest Head, and there build the terminus and village which is now Windermere (Town). Since Wordsworth's time several railway projects to span the distance between Windermere and Keswick have come forward, but financial support has been lacking. I fear to risk prophecy, but unless some stupendous change takes place, such as the discovery of precious and useful minerals among the mountain strata, the road is likely to carry all the services which the Lake Country requires. The Lake steamers are out of use, except during the holiday season.

Lowwood is still a pier for the Lake steamers, though "Calls when required" is now its fate in the time-tables. In that it is luckier than the Ferry Hotel, where the steamer pier was condemned as unsafe. The establishment of the Lake steamers raised the usual dispute against vandalism. I heard the old arguments trotted out a few years back when the horsed coaches gave way to motor-buses; also when speed-boats and hydroplanes appeared on the lake. Often when reading old newspaper files I am convinced that "great minds think alike", for I have been tempted to copy out several columns of pro and con arguments which have served again and again in the old, old disputes.

At Lowwood Hotel is the third milestone from Windermere station. Beyond it are several charming bays, alongside which low walls have been built in my time. You could step off the path into the woods without the slightest trouble. My impressions may be wrong, but fifty-odd years ago we travelled nearer the breakers. Probably the road has been lifted a yard, and is less affected by flood and spray. A disused limekiln, hidden among some bushes, is a memory. The bit of wood on the right for a third of a mile was formerly open (but not public). Now iron railings have intervened for thirty years.

The first garden on the right was famous for its late and early roses: the first seemed to appear in May, and the last was still scented in mid-December. The aged owner was proud of this sheltered border, and would allow only a few windbreaks so that coach riders and people walking on the other side of the road shared his delight.

The views across the lake have changed but little: the scale is so vast that the minute specks of new residences hardly count. There is a bridge and then a descent towards Waterhead. At the foot of this

COACH AND FOUR: SURVIVOR OF THE OLD-TIME LAKELAND TRAFFIC

LIVELY WATER: TROUT FISHING AFTER HEAVY RAIN IN RIVER BRATHAY

slope there used to be access to the lake, but now the gamut of a hideous petrol-station has to be run.

At Waterhead, the group of buildings has changed little in outer appearance : the road has been banked from wall to wall to suit the new travel, and across the strand the former row of cottages and a farm have given place to a rather straggling private hotel.

Returning to the main road, I think every yard into Ambleside has been rebuilt and regraded in my time, but it is difficult to identify any particular point. The lane which splits to the right in half a mile is said to be the original road into Ambleside, and the old town was sited along it until the new coach route was cut direct to the market-place. From the market cross, the ancient road went across the Stock to the old church, then dropped to the left for Rydal and Gras-mere. The only alteration I can recall is the cutting out of a bus station behind the Queen's Hotel. The funny bridge with its two-storeyed cottage over the Stock has been isolated. I am told that it was originally built as a waiting-room for guests at a mansion (which has disappeared entirely) across the stream. Servants and baggage waited below and gentry above until the coach drove up.

Beyond the fifth milestone the road changes have been gradual : as each building came into existence the frontage was set back. The heavy traffic of today demands every inch of road surface at times, and at the end of the section, beyond the old Methodist Chapel, the rocks within a curve have been cut away. To Scandale beck, there is a new foot-path outside the original stone wall, and other sections are treated in the same way where possible. At the meeting of Rydal and Rothay becks, a light foot-bridge has been thrown across the former rill to render the way safer and easier for all.

When I first saw it Rydal was pretty much the same as it is today, and the same applies to the road past Wordsworth's seat and the bay of the water-lilies. It is narrow and tortuous, and quite dangerous when traffic moves thick and fast. From the top of the next hill, past Nab Cottage, a new road has been constructed which touches the shore of Rydal Water, and cuts out two awkward and narrow bends, particularly past some farm buildings. The water-trough at the seventh milestone is little changed, but on a dry windy day its surface is scummed with black, nasty smuts. I have had many a drink of water there with my first meal, at four a.m. after a midnight start for Keswick. Later in the day, the air was choked with dust.

Up White Moss the road has doubled in width or in use ; here again it is not easy to see the new engineering. The little shanty next the quarry remains unchanged, but the Wishing Gate road is no longer a green lane. The old path by White Moss tarn is greatly trodden by

B

ramblers who use it as a pleasant return from Red Bank over the foot-bridge, and to Grasmere by Dove Cottage.

The next mile through the woods between the two lakes and ending at White Rock shows no great change, but forty years back there was a green belt on either side of the coach-tracks. The Prince of Wales Hotel, from this side, does not seem to have changed, but there are more houses on the hill-side about Town End than there used to be, and I miss the old blacksmith's forge, the hammers of which rang at early day when I walked through to Keswick.

Now we come to Grasmere, where all roads end. I used to hear gossip that Rigg's coaches claimed to be "Royal", with their drivers in red, because they had the mail contract between Windermere, Bowness, Ambleside and Grasmere. The letters over Dunmail Raise, to Wythburn, Legburthwaite, the hamlet at the foot of Thirlmere and Armboth, were carried at first by a man on foot; later by a cyclist postman. There was no carrying of letters to Keswick by the daily coach—and in winter there was no coach at all.

From Wordsworth's fountain at Town End a direct road goes up the east of the vale to the Swan Hotel and Keswick. It was formerly a grassy lane, with little hummocks where the drains and culverts passed. It is now a main road with the hedges bulged away by cars and charas. In Grasmere the bridge at the church has been reinforced and widened again and again; a slice has been taken off the Vicarage garden; the awful twist into Red Lion Square remains, but the exit is easier, and the way past the village hall must have been gradually doubled. White Bridge and its approaches have been altered within the past ten years, and now there is only about three hundred yards (past the cemetery) below the requisite width.

From the Swan Hotel, the road has been widened again and again. The Travellers' Rest Inn is the same outside, but altered within; Tongue Ghyll Bridge has been set back; the old road under Helm from Grasmere village is altered where it touches the Keswick road. At Town Head the old toll house is in process of burial in efforts to ease the gradient beyond. This is the steepest part of Dunmail Raise. In the old days the coachmen expected the active among passengers to get down and walk. The road was scored on the other side with the skidpans of descending carriages. The old mine tunnel in Seat Sandal is still moist and dirty. Last summer some youths emerged from the shaft as I came up; they had gone to the far end of the working and were still undecided whether the seams were of iron, copper or lead ore. I made the same crawl long years back, with a stub of candle for illumination, and a nervous dalesman as support. He wanted to turn back in ten yards from the start.

We are now high on Dunmail Raise: if the talk should turn on possible Roman roads from Dictis camp at the head of Windermere to the ports of the Solway coast, it is not difficult to trace a possible route along a belt of hard land at the foot of the eastern-side hills. I have often complained that Dunmail Raise is a draughty place: the dame who lived at the highest cottages declined to keep poultry because the wind "wad bla' 'em to the divvle an they sud leuk oot on a breezy day". I suggested that it might be pleasant, on that snowy day, to follow them a mile or two to such warmer zones, but she thought it was just my impidence! The road up the deep trough between Seat Sandal and Steel Fell has been flattened and straightened again and again, and I have lost two little hummocks altogether.

I had my fortune told, years ago, on Dunmail Raise under circumstances which smack very much of George Borrow. A band of gipsies had been camped there as usual, and the children swarmed out to beg as the coaches and carriages passed. As I came up a small child, running in behind one conveyance, fell and might have been run over. There were yards to spare in front of the leaders in the next coach, and the horses were at the walk, so there was nothing splendid or daring in picking up the wee mite. Coachee rather too forcibly put my feelings: "Those —— (bairns) are a —— nuisance, tumbling right in front of my hosses!" And a German lady laboriously pronounced sentence: "It verry brav and glor-rious wass," before Coachee, with a wave of his whip to me, sent the horses along.

There had been a volley of shouts to and from the gipsy camp, and now I was the centre of some chattering Romany men, women and children. It was soon borne in on me that I was accredited with a deed of no small importance. Different men, one a big, burly chap fit to eat me, took my elbows, and with gentle force I was conducted to the central tent of the group. I don't remember hearing much English nor, when I made out the presence of an ancient crone, smoking a short black pipe in the back of this tent, was I greatly impressed. But the others talked hurriedly and apparently to the point in Romany, their remarks cut into by her whip-like queries, and then the old lady deigned to address me. My bodyguard side-stepped, and I was allowed the full force of her shrill but apparently benevolent remarks. The situation was not without its humour. The old lady, seeing that I didn't understand a single word, screamed something loudly, and the chatter behind me instantly ceased. A gorgeously dressed lady of a younger generation (by the way, she was smoking a small black cheroot) came to the front and began to act as interpreter. Not being a novelist writing my reminiscences, not yet the hero of a novel, I have long since forgotten her exact words, but they should have been majestic—I had saved an important member of the family, the seventh child of a seventh child repeated seven times, and the head of the family thanked me in a farrago of laudatory terms linked up with rotten grammar and a garnishing of slang. What would I accept as reward? A bag of money was produced from somewhere, and a stream of yellow coins slowly trickled on to a red cotton handkerchief.

When I had convinced the interpreter that the whole business was so much nonsense to me, she was a bit perturbed and began to explain that the old dame was a sort of queen and would be affronted if I did not accept reward. I replied, "Bosh." There was an interchange of speeches (by the way, I am sure that the regal grandmother understood English, but did not deign to speak it), and as a final offer the old lady was made to suggest that I might have my fortune told. The words were first pronounced in Romany, then in English, the interpreter adding that it was a great honour indeed for a queen to offer. She was descended from Lot's wife or Eve, I'm not sure which, or was it the Queen of Sheba? As a thunderstorm was breaking just at that moment over the fells, I was not sorry of an excuse for shelter. And here is my revelation of the next half-hour. The tent was cleared, the old gipsy moved her stool so that she sat, a bent old witch, between me and the triangle of doorway; to right, to left of her, the darkness of storm-clouds hiding distant lake and hills, then the silver trees of lightning, the grey waves of rain, the final clearing of the air, the distant bar of sunshine, and then the clear, bright sunshine of afternoon. And the thunder grumbled and rattled and crashed and echoed the while the queen spoke slow her readings of my hands and face, her companion in low voice interpreting to me:

"You may hope to live long, for the days of ill-health are behind. You may hope to rise in the world, but it will be slowly, for you have too much pride and will not bend where you should. You never will be lucky in money matters, picking up money which you have not sown, but you will never be without money or dis-hon-our-ab-ly" (I remember that word well, every syllable was pronounced separately) "in debt. Whatever you want, you will have to work for and work hard for, but you will get it in good time. Hills and rocks and mountains, mountains and rocks and torrent-sides will be your pleasure and your fortune, but not for gold, not for gold."

And at this point the old lady ceased; she seemed to go into a rapt reverie, and the younger one gripped my elbow, saying softly, "Come: there is no more that tongue can utter." In two minutes I was out of sight of the encampment, swinging down the rain-washed road on my homeward journey.

Fifty-odd years on—well, I can afford to confess that the old gipsy

queen was pretty correct in her reading of my character and fortune.
I still have to work hard, and there is still much to acquire, much to do.

Beyond Raise Bridge, Manchester Corporation remodelled the
road, and it now flows easily down the west side for a mile before
crossing to the right. The original road went to the right almost at
once, and it can be traced, though cut off by gates at each end. There
is a bridge rifted by some forgotten flood on the line of the old route.
Forty years ago this remained the road, and last September I again
used it, locating the stumps of two big Scots pines and the inscription
let into the ruined wall—

30th 9mo 1843.
Fall'n from his fellow's side,
    The steed beneath is lying:
In harness here he died;
    His only fault was dying.
                    W.B.

A horse belonging to William Ball, a Quaker friend of Wordsworth,
who also lived at Rydal, fell dead on the road and is commemorated.

For years Manchester has steadily increased the acreage of conifers
at Thirlmere. They have planted right into the Raise pass. As a
shepherd lad said to me, "Thirlmere's become a dowlish shop," with
dingy conifers. No, I fear that I cannot thank the Corporation for the
dull, if useful, mantle which now almost covers all the narrow meadows
and climbs high on the fell-sides. Still, the traveller of my boyhood
had no chance of seeing wild red deer, both stags and hinds, which
have settled down among the trees and made a "forest" of Helvellyn.
With a bit more luck in bird protection, we shall have more ravens
and maybe eagles returning to the cliffs in Naddle and similar places.

Forty years ago the waters of Thirlmere never lapped the roadside
walls—now in time of high rains there is a narrow strip between the
road and Helvellyn side, and Wythburn's inn and the vicarage has been
closed. The church of Wythburn remains, so does the schoolhouse,
but Armboth and other farms have been flooded out, and only the
flock-owner at West Head remains as Master of Helvellyn, with his
sheep ranging from the Sticks Pass to Sergeant Man at the back of
Langdale Pikes ten mountain miles away.

When I first knew the mountain-side above Wythburn it was open
grass and scree; now the ghyll past the school is choked with plantations, and it is easier to follow the old "pony-track" rather than attempt
a straight line to the ridge of the mountain as we used to do. Despite
the extinction of the Nag's Head, this path is still used by hundreds of
ramblers every year.

Going on towards Keswick, it was still possible in my young days to leave the new road, and to drop past the shells of some cottages and climb back to the road a mile beyond the "Rock of Names". It would be a tough scramble through woods today. The neck between Thirlmere and Legburthwaite is crossed by many roads and paths, some of which are primitive indeed. The road which descends to the King's Head has been widened within recent years, and some curves which I recollect in early cycling years have disappeared altogether. You can see the long straight from top to bottom; the road beyond the hotel has changed little in direction, but there are no longer evidences of flooding such as we knew in the old times.

That reminds me that the road over Dunmail Raise and on the neck past Wythburn was often tufted with grass after winter. There were patches of mud, moss and stones squirted from the marshes and hill-sides. I have seen flocks of sheep snatching at such tufts as they were leisurely driven from Hawkshead in Lancashire to the Helvellyn pastures for summer. I doubt whether the right to graze on these fells has been exercised for many a year.

I have a recollection that the lofty bridge over the Thirlmere outlet at Smurthwaite was built in my very early years, or why should I have a memory of coaches galloping down to a narrow arch or hummock, and springing the steep slope on the Keswick side? I am content to leave it at that.

The last miles into Keswick usually found me getting my "second breath" as a tramper, and perhaps my memory is not so clear. Probably too all these roads were still new roads, for Manchester's big enterprise had just been finished, and many miles had been rebuilt and relaid both here and in the Vale of St. John after the extremely heavy traffic had passed. Dalehead Hall on the shore of Thirlmere was then said to be kept open for the use of inspecting committees, and Cumberland neighbours would see to it that the approaches from Keswick were kept beyond criticism. Manchester had proved to be a good and generous customer in all transactions with the northern country.

The coming of the motor-bus caused changes on the final miles in to Keswick, and Nest Brow, which rises on the west side of Naddle, was straightened out, together with the twisted lanes. There were extremely narrow places, particularly that section between St. John in the Vale vicarage and the crossing of Shoulthwaite beck which needed remedy. More than one chara or bus turned over while trying to take the corner at the foot of Nest Brow at high speed.

The road-verges between Nest Brow and Keswick, which were once full of flowers and grasses, have shrunk almost out of sight. At the last milestone, it was usual to drive the winding and steep coach-road down into the market-place of Keswick, for Chestnut Hill was a grassy farm lane at all pitches and angles. Today the old coach-road is known mostly to ramblers, and they find it steep. The Chestnut Hill and Brigham route is safer and in the long run quicker for motors.

Is there anything to say about the road old and new within the town of Keswick? The entrances to the market-places are difficult as ever, but there is now a chance of cutting from the Penrith or Brigham road to the Cockermouth road by a back street and avoiding the worst tangle. Like Ambleside, Keswick has been town-planned, and mighty highways exist on paper which will cut out the tangled knots and allow swift and sure access to other radiating roads. Keswick will be by-passed to north to join the Ambleside, Penrith, Carlisle and Cocker-mouth roads; and on the south to take the Ambleside, Penrith and Carlisle traffic into Borrowdale without any inconvenience. Against this, Ambleside is threatened with a big trunk-road up the valley which will draw long-distance visitors away from the shops and hotels and cafés.

When I tramped these long miles, such prospects would have interested me but little; to see much, to hear little, to think of past and present, not the future, would now be my desire. The horn of the red-coated mail-coach on Dunmail Raise sends my mind back to the battle days of Briton and Saxon there. I wonder what revolutions the future has in store for the great main road through the Lake District.

"Coachee"

Though the great coaching days in England ended with the coming of railways, in the Lake District horse-teams continued to work until the invasion of motor-cars and buses. Even yet a few relics of the horsed turn-outs appear about Ambleside, Coniston and Grasmere, where some beautiful scenery is not yet "developed" by modern roads. By pushing a macadam motor-road across Honister pass, the Cumberland County Council struck the death-knell of the last horsed run, the Buttermere Round. No horses can keep back a laden coach on a hard surface with a pitch of one in four-and-a-half behind them.

I am interested in the old coachmen: "Coachees" they were inti-mately called. Some of them wore Rigg's red-coats because that firm held the contract for the Royal Mail. Other firms provided their men with varying gear, but practically all had the white top hat. This hat old Jack turned to use when making up the day's accounts. He would throw all the coins he had collected from many pockets on to the flat top of some bin, then begin to share them, throwing an equal number into the top hat for the boss, and returning the others to his pockets for himself. At the end he carried the hatful of coins to the kitchen, where it was accepted as final payment.

Some of the exquisites had their driving-gloves of otter skin, and were proud of them. "The gloves of an otter are the best fortification for your hands that can be thought of against wet weather," wrote Izaak Walton, three centuries ago.

There was Coachee Bill, who "stood by" his team all winter, and was ready to drive even a dogcart anywhere. In February he used to begin plaiting new lashes for his whip; he had a great belief that a slice of fat bacon, fastened by a bit of string inside the collar, would ward off all the sore throats and colds in the world, but others were shy of the oily fancy.

There was John Sheldon, who drove the "mail coach" between Keswick and Windermere, and knew every hill and person on the 21 miles. His talk was continuous, interspersed with hails to friends in distant fields, a few words of caution, encouragement and gentle reprobation for his team. After John had left the big run, he was for years engaged in a summer tour from Troutbeck station, on the Keswick-Penrith line, to Patterdale. John was fond of comic anecdotes, and even made rough-and-ready rhymes as he tooled his team through the dales.

With John disappeared a type of Coachee which was never replaced. Later recruits were always fearful that a threatened railway would pass through Grasmere and Dunmail Raise to Keswick, and they spent their winters working horse-trams in Lancashire and Yorkshire towns. Most of them never returned to work in the dales.

There were amateurs such as Parson Bird, who were well up to the work. He would usually handle the ribands over the Raise, and be chaffed unmercifully because of thus driving the "Cuckoo", for so the coach was called.

Bird was so good-hearted a gentleman that when the regular coachman of the Keswick mail broke his leg he took the place for six weeks, and collected the fees for the unfortunate man. A story is told of a lady giving the parson-coachman half a crown at the end of the journey one afternoon, and being introduced to him at a ball the same evening. He at once asked for a dance, but she was highly indignant that a coachman should so presume. However, the matter was explained, and to such satisfaction that not only did she dance, but eventually became Mrs. Bird.

Was it one of our Lakeland coachees who allowed a noble lord (who was a good whip) to take the reins? At the end, his lordship said, "Please to remember the coachman?" Coachee replied, "Yes, I will; if you'll remember the guard?" "Right; he shall have double what you tip me." Coachee promptly handed him a five-pound note, so that after sharing with the guard he was £2 10s. in pocket.

A similar coachee had a reputation for simple living as well as a civil tongue for all comers. Of him, a critical fellow of the whip trade said, "If Coachee didn't live on potato skins and worn't such a one for licking folks's boots, he'd be perfect." But Coachee took care of his pence, retired, and after a comfortable ten years ambling round a big hotel, left a comfortable fortune to his family.

One old coachee got a fright. The mail from Keswick, coming down Nest Brow, collided wth a pony-chaise, with two middle-aged men in it. The vehicle and pony were knocked through the wall, and one of the gentlemen picked himself up, and said, in a solemn way, "I shall have this matter thoroughly investigated." David Johnson, the driver of the mail, pulled up sharp, with face pale as death—"Good God! It's Master Wadsworth."

Wordsworth was not much hurt; as David said when recounting the episode, "No, sir; thank Heaven for that! But I never heard a body's tongue sweer gladlier though, for I thowt we'd kilt the poit." Apparently the off-wheeler of the coach had tossed his head and got the bit entangled in the pole-hook, and in consequence Coachee had lost control at a critical moment.

The last of the old Coachees has passed away. Whether the new road transport will breed a definite type of man like the old white-hatted "whip" remains to be seen. However, there is no appearance as yet of a specialist and interesting character.

The Yard of Tin

Though the coachmen of old are dead,
    Though the guards are turned into clay,
You will still remember the yard of tin,
    And the mail of the olden day.

Yes, we do remember, though nowadays the motor-car has usurped every road-service of the post-office. You have to go into very remote places to find the old one-horse trap tracking across broken moorland rocks to some knot of lost farms. And the passing of the "yard of tin" is complete. Ben the guard no longer toots them out of the way—potters' carts, farm wagons, flocks of sheep, droves of cattle and horses—even pigs and geese and the erratic pedestrian who does not immediately look upwards at the thunder of the approaching team. The motor-car never rouses the fine spirit of the old coaches:

"Yes, it was a thick morning: the horn was going all along the lake, and through the pass, and even then we had to watch for a smash-up."

The modern motorist plunges faster, hits harder, and is more sudden in his damage. But he has no Yard of Tin to herald his way. A snorting, coughing reedy siren should clear the way—but it isn't a pleasant sound. The first motor-coaches in the Lake Country are said to have had mechanical horns simulating the first five notes of "D'ye ken John Peel?" It might be so—I never recognized the lilt. The motorist who carries such a bugle is a man of mark: "Here he comes again, with his own blooming orchestra." We never had such insult to the old yard of tin. "There's Bobby's horn," said the dweller on the Furness shore, "that means drinking-time—half past ten." A call on the horn was distinctive: the hooter of the motor-car is commonplace, vulgar, and you cannot distinguish the honk of His Majesty's Mail from any of the thousand cars rushing along the upper road.

The Christmas Mail

After all, many who are still nimble veterans remember the Christmas mails which were brought by the old horse-coaches to isolated villages and hamlets in Scotland, Wales, and England. A day or two ago one sped rapidly over eighty miles of the great Telford road, between Shrewsbury and Holyhead, great sections of which used to depend on "coaches" for communication between the sparse railway stations. There used to be cushions of moss on the road above Pentre Voelas, and over the pass of Llanberis. Still better, one recalls the Christmas-time appearance of great coaching roads across the Lake District. Romance indeed—often enough the drivers who brought Christmas to Ambleside and Grasmere wore the vermilion jackets of the "Royal Mail", and their four horses had a rare load of folks returning for the holiday at home, for scrambles among the rocks and ridges, as well as bringing our precious missives.

At Christmas-time the whisky flowed like water round the postman who brought up the mail, be the day frosty or dirty or merely unpleasant. One has known the Christmas mail come through the pass on a day of raging snow, with drifts among the wheels, extra horses, and a postillion on the leaders. It was such a morning that old Jim alluded to when we were driving through the dark morning to Grasmere. "They tells me that motors are going to be put on this job; but, believe me, it can't be done. Them hosses can either see, or hear, or smell their way in the worst storm as ever blew, and they never swerve a foot from their place on the road."

Many a Christmas mail had old Jim brought to the village, and the way his mail slipped about the ice-bound roads was something to remember. In these days racing motor-cyclists dash round dirt-tracks and skid their corners; wonders never cease, but old Jim and other drivers of the Christmas mails half a century or more ago did the same thing, and a plunging horse-team and hummocky roads added sensation. To me, old Jim, who drove until the last horse-mail in Westmorland was swept away by the motor-van, was a link with the great coach-drivers of the past. He was a stable-boy before the first railway to Scotland ran across the moors, and he saw the rapid extinction of long-distance road travel. He alleged that the change came more suddenly than the motor-car, which displaced the horse. "What, man, one year there was only talk; next there was a thousand navvies at work on the hills; and in one week there was no more passengers for the coaches, and they were taken off the road."

After all, a century covers the whole history of steam-driven locomotion; prior to that anyone who wished to travel fast and far had either to hire a horse or sit behind a team. The entire business of the country travelled along the coach-roads. Heavy goods and slow passengers went by wagon. And the tracks called roads—why, a century and a half ago Arthur Young denied their existence as possible through-routes. Mud seemed to have stopped travellers even between London and Kensington.

Royalty, nobles, and the rich had their private coaches, even in Queen Elizabeth's time, but the public service which gradually built up Christmas on the road did not begin until much later. Oxford was two days from London, and it is stated that pedlars and packmen walked alongside the travelling coaches and offered their wares. What an opportunity for a Christmas bazaar! In 1754 a Manchester firm "undertook" that their conveyance would reach London in four and a half days. It was not until 1784 that the Christmas mail, such as it was, went by coach instead of by postboys and mounted couriers. In August of that year the "new mail diligence" ran from London to Bath between eight at night and daylight next morning. John Palmer caused time and punctuality to appear on the road; the mails must start prompt and run to the minute, summer and winter, day and night, storm and calm alike. And a coachman who received his mails late was expected to make up lost time on his stage. The Edinburgh mail ultimately ran its 400 miles to London in 40 hours—and some of the coaches became so punctual that the cottagers and villagers set their clocks by the minute of their passing. The Glasgow-Carlisle coach averaged $11\frac{1}{2}$ miles per hour.

Storm often delayed, but it rarely stopped the Christmas mail altogether. The great crimson conveyance, with its powerful lamps, its good teams and skilful driver, kept going at all costs. The terrific storm of December, 1836, tested the road users terribly; for days on end London was isolated from the provinces.

A turkey famine threatened, and the coach-guards and others who brought up birds from the country made good profits. Three months later the post-office was circularizing its officers as to coaches which were still absent from the yards and were presumably over-whelmed in deep snow. The guards had a fierce time of it, for the mails were their personal concern; if the coach ditched or stuck in a drift the guard had to take a horse and ride on with the mail-bags into the storm. Sometimes this meant the risk of death. I have stood on the old Edinburgh turnpike near Moffat and looked up the ladder-like ascent to the moor where the guard and driver of the Dumfries and Edinburgh Royal Mail coach died in 1831. They had taken the mail-bags on their own shoulders after the road was drifted too much for wheels, and went forward on foot until they were overwhelmed.

One hears again in memory the echoes of the yard of tin twanging as through the darkness the old coach again makes its way past Rydal Mount in the morning of Christmas; one sees again the faint shadow of coach lamps looming through the night mist under the hills and alongside Grasmere's lake; and one has just a touch of regret that the old romance, which in childhood days meant so much for some of us who were reared far away from railways, can never come again with the Christmas mail.

CHAPTER TWO

COTTAGE ANGLERS

A Successful Lass—Out With the Bracken Clock—Varying Trout—October Spawning

I WAS born in a hamlet in a county of trout-streams, and I have always loved the silver-blue fishes spotted with a crimson hail, and the clear waters they haunt. Like other cottage anglers I started to catch them with primitive equipment: I remember the whippy ashplant to the top of which was fastened a few yards of real fishing-line found in a bush after a flood. We tried to make our hooks, but failed. I paid a penny for the hook with which my first trout was really captured. I doubt whether modern lads of the trout-streams have such fun!

Most of us old-timers learnt to catch trout with ramshackle tackle. A rod was not considered worn-out until its staggered appearance was obvious to any lad with twopence to spend. I paid a whole shilling, saved over many weeks of self-sacrifice, for my first rod, and then had to hide it in the blacksmith's shop to escape my maternal critic. She was obsessed with the idea that any art and pursuit which could be practised without fussiness was a waste of time. "And Satan still finds evil things for idle hands to do."

I got back my shilling from my first fish, which a parson's wife bought by the river-side. She had seen me at work with the fish, and was imperious. "I want that fish; it's Easter Sunday tomorrow. I'll give you a shilling a pound for it." She opened her purse and took out a silver coin. "It looks more than a pound weight, so if you come to the parsonage tonight I will pay you the difference, if there is any." And off she went with my prize.

Why did I decide to waive all further claims? For one thing I had to tramp home, about six miles, and get in by eight o'clock. Moreover, if the fish weighed less than a pound when it got to the scales the lady might want some pence back. I did not risk the claim.

In a few years I left the water-side village with the trout glancing in pools almost reachable from some cottage windows. Why did crippled old Tom who hated the name of trout have the window with a real opening pane, and why did all the windows of Sporting Jim face towards the road and not the river? There's a mystery for you!

Now and again I return to the old village, but no fishing is done by the lads. The best stream is rented and preserved by a club of four or five rods, and the rest is held by farmers who let their untenanted cottages by the week in spring and summer, giving angling rights off their own fields. The only satisfaction is that the offcome holiday-makers get very few fish.

Being barred from a share in the river, I go and look at the outfits of my friends who have managed to keep up angling in a stream or two of the great estate on which they are employed. It's an ancient and ungrudged privilege, and one which makes for a happy village life.

Jim the careful angler never adds an ounce to the weight of his outfit; he never adds an item to the list. As each purchase is made, some crumpled or overworked object is either sold out or destroyed.

"If it won't mend, I won't keep it," is his simple maxim.

George, on the other hand, has an attic in his house which he dare not enter. He reckons that the furnishing of this with part-used tackle must have cost him about sevenpence a week. A penny a day for anglers' waste may not seem much, but it makes a big sum in a series of years. George's fault is that he cannot resist a "new idea" which costs but a trifle, and has usually to be discarded after making an experimental appearance alongside the stream. His actual working out-fit is more primitive than that shown by John.

Ike has a corner cottage, and tells strangers that he can drop a line from his own garden. He can, but the water in front is just a clean-washed surface, as a rule, about four inches deep, and there is never a trout to be seen. Ike's rod comes out chiefly when the river is in summer flood, and the fish go mad in their chase of worms. He doesn't believe in reg'lar fishing, condemns it as a waste of time and brains. At which we agree that Ike is sensible; he never had brains to waste. His gear is awful stuff; neglected, never looked at from summer to summer, and with the chance of any big fish breaking clean away, and losing half the rod in mid-flood.

Young Tommie is grey of head, and the best fisher of us all. He got belted in school years ago when he whispered too audibly that he wasn't going to stop in after school. There was good fishing up the beck, and he knew where the postman on his rounds had hidden his rod. Tommie acquired his sport from anglers who had a love for it, but Harry gets his from father and grandfathers to whom our streams were a passion. They all might have been good workmen at steady wages if they had left the fishing alone. Instead of that they were casual labourers, for who knew when they might drop the job they had in hand and take the rest of the day or week for fishing? My mother looked upon the men of her time as terrible examples of improvidence. But I wonder if she was really and truly right. Somehow or other they managed to keep clear of that village bugbear, the workhouse, and the last of the old brigade had his share of the Old Age Pension before he cast his line into the river pools and streams for the last time.

What am I writing about? I began with cottage anglers and their tackle, but have wandered a good deal. Still, pardon me, I have the flash of moving streams, of trout alert and turning in the deep waters, and many a boyhood memory of the youthful old, old hamlet.

Why does one river village breed its scores of youthful anglers while at the next hamlet, a mile up or downstream, the natives never handle a rod and line? Angling curates and schoolmasters fail to infect the second village with any enthusiasm. The people look askance on water-side sport, and comment on misplaced zeal. "Oh, you're in the wrong parish now. They'd suit you better at the lower bridge. The folks there is allus fishin'."

Frankly there is no good explanation. Here are two places remarkably alike in history, situation and opportunity, yet one looks upon the river as a low, unclean and even obscene place. You find such villages in pairs and contrasts on the Welsh Dee, Irish Erne, Scottish Tweed, and, in former years, on English Dove, Wye and Teme. There is precious little good trout-fishing available, without fee, for cottagers and cottage lads after the clubs have had their way in rural England.

Old John of Angling declares that the rodless village was once afflicted by a revival. After that the good folk declined to take any part in wicked sport. "We can fish right through their village, and never a one asks 'What sport?' They won't buy trout because they have seen them killed, and they are sick with the pain." John's Revival theory is rather feeble; Angling has the skeletons of three sprawling chapels built after different outbursts of religious fervour.

I offer an alternative theory. Maybe Angling had its sport engrained in flesh and blood because it stands close to the ruins of an ancient monastery. Under the Old Faith, Thursday's rod had to be skilfully applied, or Friday's fare would be meagre indeed. Fearing ill-luck on their own efforts, the monks encouraged their humble neighbours to catch trout and pike whenever possible. The other village was barred from river and wood because it was within the demesne of a knight of the shire, whose household did much less fasting on trout.

My experience shows that a non-sporting community may be worthy and staid, but there is life and joy in a village of anglers. "We take no interest in it," is an ingrained excuse. I admit that out-of-doors Angling is picturesque rather than tidy, but where are there neater interiors?

I believe in heredity and environment. Bring up the bairn of angling family in an angling village, and, if a man-child, he will join the craft and become a master. Our history has never named a female lover of water-side sport; the tragedy would be too great for written or spoken words. The lasses must hide their skill or divert it to home neatness. Where can you see such neat knots and repairs as in Angling village?

A Successful Lass

I have just watched an Angling tragedy. Like a Chinese play it has lasted seven years, but the characters are the same two. Man and Maid throughout, turning to Bride, Wife and now Mother. Janet defied convention; village lasses had hitherto taken no share in the angling, but she went out with her lover, shared his rod, and caught

fish. Jackie the carpenter lad then made her a light lancewood
wand, with delicate reel and tackle "fit for a queen", said the village.

"Noo ye're fit up," Jackie laughed as Janet made her first cast
with her new possession. It was a drake which just touched the far
side of the stream, and rolled off the grass into the water—to be taken
by a nice trout waiting below!

The village dames were truly scandalized when Janet fought and
killed the renowned three-pounder in the bridge pool. Every angler
in the village had trailed flies, floated minnows, bobbed grubs and
worms, and had spun varied baits before the monster—and it only
grew fatter, bigger and more desirable. Janet had come down at
dusk, and flicked her fly gently across and under the alders, the great
fish's favourite haunt. In a moment the trout had sucked down the
tiny fly; the girl's wrist turned and flicked the barb into her monster.
In a moment the lancewood tip was dancing and bending, and Janet had
started the great battle. She was determined to kill and land her
fish alone. "Keep off, Jackie; it's mine!" she screamed. "I'll either
kill it or loss it!"

The village inn was empty in five seconds when somebody clattered
past—"Janet's ho'd o't' big troot." Even blind Simon clamoured to
be guided out, "If I can't see, let me listen."

"Wait till I get my apron off," said the landlord.

"Wait be dashed; it'll be over afore you can mannish that," snapped
Simon.

So the inn-keeper came out just as he was. In thirty years he had
never appeared off his own doorstep in his insignia.

Down in the bronze dusk, there was one white patch—Janet's face.
There was a tense hush-hush of parted water as the fish curved and
swept about the pool, and after each struggle the reel gained its inches
of line. "She'll get it," whispered Simon, his ears acute to many things
not noted by the folks with vision. "It's tiring." But it took twenty
good minutes to bring the trout to the surface, and to run it on to the
shingles at the girl's feet. Just as it touched the shallow, the girl
swung out the landing-net and neatly enmeshed it. Victory was secure.
Janet neither fainted nor yet yelled "Halloo" like certain modern
Dianas. She merely picked up the victim, looked at it in the dying
light, and asked Jackie, "Who shall weigh it?" And she endeavoured
to dodge back into the meadows when the bridge was "wick wi' folk".
Angling village had turned out, and they gave her the angler's cheer. But
after weighing to the grocer's last quarter-ounce, she and Jackie disappeared in the excitement, unnoticed. The inn-keeper claimed the
trout.

"Come on; it won't be a dry customer, Isaac," he said to the grocer.

YOUNG SHEPHERD AND LAMB: SCENE ON THE TROUTBECK
(WESTMORLAND) FELLS

WORDSWORTH'S GRASMERE, WITH GORSE IN BLOSSOM AND ROAD CLIMBING DUNMAIL RAISE
IN BACKGROUND

Simon the blind one still says, "It teuk a lot o' free ale to wet that troot, but it was worth it."

Now where comes the promised tragedy? Angling village made Janet a bold adventuress, a terrible example, and the lasses shunned the water-side more than ever. There is no life partnership made in Angling since Janet and Jackie strolled the meadows. "Aye," says their son, "and it's many a good swish I have had from the top joint of my mother's old rod."

Out With the Bracken Clock

In the low country the angler gives pride of place to the mayfly among his summer lures for lusty trout. Here, in the recesses of the hills, the swarming bracken clock is far more favoured. The beetle with bright green metallic wing-cases creeps on every grass tuft, flies in every drift of the breeze, and is always a shocking traveller, a worse aeronaut. It is always capsizing in the grass, it blunders in to one's face, and even into one's mouth if too much talking is a vice.

Thousands of these bracken clocks fall into our wee river pools, and lie sprawling on the glassy surface of the tarns. Their wings are very weak and uncertain at best. It is the time of feasting for our trout; noses just push through the waterskin, there is a gulp and the beetle disappears. Sometimes a wee bead of water rolls awhile on the surface, then slips back into its element.

The bracken clock hatches in myriads; one hour not an insect is visible; next they are clinging everywhere among the coarse grass and fern, and launching on their futile aerial voyages. Long ago the pipits and other birds tired of them; the trout, however, will feast until the last beetle has gone. And then for a month they sulk. Our local anglers say that the hard elytra or wing-cases cause scour, after which the trout is a cautious feeder for weeks. He is not going to risk a new-lined stomach on any unruly fare. Well, lucky the creature which has the power of refurnishing its digestive interior, that's all.

The angler is interested in the bracken clock because, during its season, the mountain fishes will look at no other lure. The beetle is less than half an inch long and can be used on either stream or tarn. In the former it is simply dibbled into each pool, walking upstream. One gets a merry toll of fishes; luckily they are small in size, for many are hooked in rock troughs where a net could not be used, and where there is not an inch of shingle for landing.

On a tarn, the bracken clock is more difficult to manipulate. Still, it is a fairly tough customer, and with a little practice a reasonable amount of line can be got out without flicking the fly off. There is a good imitation if you care not for the live insect. This little copy is so balanced that it floats right side up no matter how you cast it. Even where trout refuse it, they rarely fail to come up for a look at the strange beast. The artificial lure can be used like a floating fly if the cast is fairly well greased.

Varying Trout

Why do the trout of our British waters vary so greatly in colour and character? The other morning I fished a mile of Yorkshire stream where every trout was richly coloured, had red edges to its fins and was an elegant fish indeed. The water-side was in keeping—clear water, beautiful gravel runs; pools which mirrored the glory of the sky, and never a dark nook. Nor was it a hungry stream, for many an insect floated into it from the moors. The next mile showed me no other than normal fish—and had I gone downstream a dozen miles I might have caught the alder trout, a sad sort of brute decked in grey and black which dwells among the roots of trees in pools and which the old naturalists fondly believed to be a separate species. All this happened on one river.

In a mountain tarn of Mardale, Westmorland, the trout are often splashed with great red spots; in another near Wasdale Head, they are said to have golden fins, but I have only caught ordinary trout in that water. Red tarn on Helvellyn has a "silver trout", but this is identified with the skelly or gwyniad of Ullswater. Ireland has several curious types—the gillaroo has a wonderful stomach and bright peach and light orange sides. It feeds largely on molluscs and needs all the powers of its quasi-gizzard to reduce these to amenable food. The slob is a fish which has lost its characteristic colour in estuary water and is a sort of creamy grey with black and red spots. The black-finned trout is found in Wales, Ireland and Scotland; and there is the Loch Stennis or yellow trout from Orkney, which is a sort of estuary giant, for the tide flows into part at any rate of its haunt.

Another big trout is the grey or great lake variety which has been called *Salmo Ferox*, but is still identified with some difficulty. It is essentially a lover of deep water, and grows to great weight—however, no one ever caught a wee *ferox*, and therefore the variety is in dispute.

After all, there is not much to be said about these fishes. I had rather yarn about the mythical occupants of the llyns of Snowdonia. In one there are fish which are humpbacked, an accident caused by their falling in early youth over a waterfall to reach the llyn at all.

In Llyn y Cae of Cader Idris, Pennant found three varieties of trout—
dark, silvery and red-finned. The last he considered to be a distinct
species. He found too a llyn which had "a race of trouts [which I
have seen] with most deformed heads, thick, flatted and toad-shaped;
and which, probably, might give rise to the fabled accounts of the
monstrous species recorded by Giraldus." But it was Giraldus who
declared that in his day Llyn y Cwn, on Glyder Fawr, was noted for
containing three kinds of fish—trout, perch and eels—all of them
monocular, wanting the left eye. Surely the most varying trout of
all.

October Spawning

Leisurely I look over the bridge at the trout in the shallow, slow-
gliding pool below. This is a favourite place, both when sport is astir
and when it is not. I certainly love to look at the trout in the off-
season and plan some subtle little campaigns for their entertainment
next summer. Somehow it does not come off, for the wary creatures
do not lie in quite the same positions.

From this height the water is crystal-clear, and the sun casts weak
ripples on the floor in imitation of June afternoon. Yet there is
change all round : a dead leaf floats past ; there is a shadow of peat in
the whirlpool ; the light is dull, and the trout move most unhappily.
They are taking little interest in food, and their gills scarcely move.
They mope as though destiny had marked them for some evil day.

The time of spawning is at hand. Between the last day of lawful
angling and today the fish have changed considerably. We found
that the last to come to the basket were getting soft of flesh, but now
the iridescence and metallic lustre of their scales is gone. There is
instead a sooty blackness spreading over the sides and throat, and
could one but handle them, the bodies would be slimy and disagreeable
to the touch. The beautiful fish one admired in high summer has
become repulsive by the time of spawning arrives.

Shortly the fish will be swimming off in couples, and they will disappear upstream for their purpose. Away in the shallows, the female
will swim over a gravelly bit where the current is brisk but not violent.
The places are traditional, and one soon finds from the chatter of
water-side folk, or just as well by keeping a bright look-out for likely
places. Having chosen a spot to her fancy, the female trout now rolls
upon her side and flaps her tail rapidly so as to fan up the grave land
excavate for herself a hollow. This trough is gradually worked deeper
and deeper, and in a day or two the female deposits such of her ova

as are ripe for shedding, usually beginning at the downstream end of the groove and working upwards.

The male, who has been in close attendance, now moves up and sheds his milt over the ova, and as both fish travel slowly upstream, the actions of their fins and tails bury the eggs as fast as they are impregnated. This process is repeated daily until all the ova are deposited. During this period the trout, unlike their kindred the salmon, feed ravenously on anything which comes down the stream, and their appetite, continuing, is rewarded by a rapid return of brilliancy to the scales. The fish, however, remain lank and emaciated until the spring warmth puts real insect food into the stream.

After the spawn is safely deposited by the fish, it is exposed to many dangers; flood may wash out the gravel bed and its precious contents or bury the whole in rotting leaves and other rubbish. Or frost may grip the land and the river run so slow that the gravel is frozen. The mere chill does not much impair the fertility of the ova, but the grinding about of icy particles is fatal. It seems almost incredible that trout should devour the spawn of their own species, yet late-comers to the breeding-places, which disturb the earlier ova by their digging and fanning, also feed on whatever the stream floats up and past. Spawning may go on for a couple of months in a big river, or where lake and river trout use the same place. Every water-bird— duck, grebe, heron, moorhen—is a peril to ova, and to the tiny fishes when hatched.

This hatching commences in about sixty days from the time of deposit—if the weather is not too frosty or the waters too warm. In either case the ova will suspend the hidden activities for a better chance. But in nine weeks from the deposit the careful observer of fish-life (who should also be an angler) will find young fry ready to burst their membranes and become little trout of the streams. In this condition they keep far away from the seniors of their kind, who will make a meal of any wanderer outside the shallows to the deeper water.

CHAPTER THREE

BY WORDSWORTH'S ROTHAY

From Seat Sandal to Windermere—The Poet's Path—As Skater—
Thomas de Quincey as 'Statesman—Westmorland and Hogarth.

THE other day I scrambled from the source of Wordsworth's
Rothay in Seat Sandal down to Grasmere : the stream is full of
beauty and history. That first ladder of boulders which starts above
the great hawthorn on Dunmail Raise is famous. Up here, says the
legend, rushed the bearers of King Dunmail's golden crown on that
disastrous day nine centuries ago when the monarch of old Cumberland
was killed by the invading Saxons.

"I will lead again," he breathed, as the bright circlet was lifted
from his brows. The warriors climbed the gorge and dropped the
crown into Grisedale tarn across the mountain, then melted into the
boiling mist, where they await his summons. And once a year, the
story goes, they become impatient and return to the earth. They arm
themselves, lift the crown from the deep water, and bear it down to the
mighty tumulus under which the King's body is buried. Thrice does
the leader strike the stones with his spear, but each time has come the
answer—"Not yet, not yet ; wait a while, my warriors." And so the
phantom army disappears into the whirling mist and darkness once
again.

It is within my personal recollection that, during the eight months
of winter, grass and moss rooted in the mud which exuded across the
road. The hollow, except for the hoarse thin voice of Rothay, is still
quiet out of the tourist season : in late April I stood here with the
returning swallows in pairs dipping past, twittering to each other as
they espied the lake beyond the pass. "Nearer home." At the same
time I watched a heron frog-hunting in a marsh, and meeting with
some success. In Wordsworth's time the heron nested on the trees of
Rydal's greatest island, but now the nearest haunts are at Wythop
above Bassenthwaite, and at Whitestock near Ulverston. On a March
midnight I have come through the pass, and heard the cries of wild
geese on their northward flight.

Nowadays the traffic across Rothay's first bridge is practically all
mechanical and without a shadow of character. I love to remember
the red-faced old Coachees who drove their spanking teams to and from
Keswick, and who always halted them for a breather at the top of the
rise. Old Joe was rather annoyed by a German lady who had spoilt his

stock stories by petulant cross-examination. "But the Helm Crag,
coachman; I never see the Lamb but only the Lion it is." "M'um,
that there's a British Lion you see; and the Lamb is now inside, eaten
while you were coming up the pass. Gee-up, you blankety blanks."

In the level trench of Dunmail, the Rothay ripples indecisively
among spits of loose shingle, dodging the little marshes where the
cotton grass has its green stars, and where the sphagnum moss bulges
up in grey and red patches. Then it slides over a steep slab of slate,
and begins to sing a low but happy song. It has started again, a real
stream down the hillside. Alongside its gorge is an old green track
which was the ancient route from Grasmere to Keswick. I don't know
when the present road by the "Travellers' Rest" was engineered, whether
in turnpike days or earlier, but this is a much older track to Keswick.

Every hundred yards the Rothay receives little becks from the
springs in Seat Sandal or Steel Fell, some large enough to burst down
the rocks in a shimmer of drops, others so thin that they merely soak
through the moss and glisten on the liverworts beneath the ledges.
Everywhere bracken, heather and bilberry clutch their roots among
shaking grass. The larch and ash have now joined the hawthorn and
the rowan, and there is a rock crevice in which is rooted a strong holly
bush. There is something else in that gaping rock—an untidy mass of
grass and moss which earlier in the year held a clutch of eggs of the
dipper or water-crow. There is ivy too, gripping the rock-end and
probably hiding the brown owl which at night patrols this hill-side. I
have heard it many a time.

I love to think that William Wordsworth and his sister Dorothy
often came this way, for it is the most beautiful water-side in the Grasmere vale, and the outward views into the green cup occupied by the lake
and fenced by green woodlands and greener mountains is marvellous
indeed. At Gillfoot the Rothay emerges into full sunshine once more,
after its wandering through brakes where the shadows lie in patches
among the netted sunshine. When Greenburn beck adds its water,
they dance along, bright but without mystery. At midnight their song
is hushed, and you hear the breeze soughing among the rocks of Helm
Crag high above. At dawn the skylarks spring up from the flower-
decked meadows and rouse the air with melody. And one hears the
sheep bleating on the hill-sides.

Every half-mile now brings in a comparatively big stream—perhaps four or five feet wide—Tongue beck from the recesses of Fairfield, Easedale beck, and then the clear stream combines and winds
round the encroaching mass of Butterlip Howe, to pass through Smithy
Bridge and to receive a last stream from Greenhead Ghyll before
encircling Grasmere village, and pausing in a deep pool outside the

kirkgarth where beneath the green yew-trees is the grave of William Wordsworth, nature-poet and lover of vale and river, and of his gentle sister Dorothy.

The last half-mile of Rothay glides smoothly and quietly through the flowered meadows to the lake. Here in high summer the marsh will be braked with purple loosestrife, with white ladies' bedstraw winding among the reeds, with tall yellow irises, with bur-reed and sword-rushes which the Grasmere bairns will weave into traditional "burdens" such as Moses' cradle-ark and the Serpent Uplifted in the Wilderness for use on Rush-bearing day, the most ancient festival of the dale.

The Poet's River

The immortal Spirit of one happy day
Lingers beside that Rill, in vision clear.

Let us continue beside Rothay, Wordsworth's Rothay, from the lake at Grasmere through many a year and season of memory. Wordsworth loved it with a devotion which lasted to the end of his long life. From the terrace garden at Rydal Mount he looked first westward to the pass through which the rivulet flows from Grasmere; then south to Windermere, in which the Rothay is finally lost.

In these six miles or so the river sings many songs, makes many changes, passes many scenes, each more lovely than the others. At Penny Rock it quietly slips from the upper lake to fill a clear trout-pool, then begins to dance, with gradually increasing spirit, down a corridor between a green slope clothed with coppice and dark rocks covered with native oaks, in which the squirrels run and leap. Here and there birch and alder show where springs have soaked the hard ground, and there are signs of foxgloves and pale golden globe-flowers among the silver-topped rampions. Here and there the current bickers over a low obtruding reef, divides round water-worn boulders, and slides over the deep holes to which in flood-time the grey lake-trout come to feed.

Beyond the White Moss foot-bridge, with the precipitous buttress of Nab Scar almost overhanging, the Rothay soon loses its energy and brilliance, sliding slow through pools and over banks of pebbles, then slower over a bar of sand to the first deep level of Rydal Water. Beyond this the stream is lost among the lofty stems of water-grass, swords of iris, lances of rushes, pink-flowered periscaria, among willows, dwarf and scant of leaf, which have rooted feebly in the matted sods over quaking ooze. In summer this is a place of colour—kingcups, buttercups and water-avens, ox-eyes, crimson loosestrife and creamy meadow-sweet, blue of forget-me-not, chocolate and ragged white of handsome bog-bean, ivory-white grass of parnassus, with red of wild roses where the ground gives sound roothold, foam of white bed-straw, and even trailers of honeysuckle where the alders are thickest. No wonder the poet loved such a place, and with his sister Dorothy made it a place of constant pilgrimage.

There are birds here: the skylark trilling in the heavens, the sand-piper with its twitter of silver bells, the dipper with vest of white and riotous song, the wagtails in dapper grey and lemon and white, swallows dipping to the insect-haunted pools. There are nesting birds too: the handsome mallard and the neat lady duck followed by her third clutch of chicks like so many balls of golden down. In the grass there are warblers: at night one hears the "fisherman's nightingale", whose notes are harsh and scolding and do not approach the true rich strains to be heard on southern streams. The tall grey heron stalks about the shallows, spearing frogs or small fishes, but for the most part pretend-ing to be utterly asleep and inert. In Wordsworth's time these birds had a colony of nests in Rydal Water's largest island, but they have long departed from a home which is no longer quiet and retired.

The genius of Wordsworth is associated with every nook along-side the Rothay. At White Moss he met with gipsy or beggar-folk and their children, saw the glow-worms and the primroses among the wet rocks. One wonders whether the sterile ground was then so brazen with ragwort in late summer: is it only fancy which declares that this awful weed is more firmly established in the Lake Country than it used to be? However, White Moss is still a place of golden gorse, blue harebells, and crimson heather.

With the dark-faced Dorothy, William often wandered round the lake; on dark winter nights their lantern was moving, rain or storm unheeding, long after the farmer-folk had gone to bed. On the shore of Rydalmere is Nab Cottage, owned for a while by De Quincey, whose opium-caused night-wanderings were haunted by fears of terrible snakes and monsters. Afterwards it was a lodging for Li'le Hartley Coleridge, whose sprees at times were just as unfortunate. Near the lake's outlet is an outcrop of rock popularly called "Wordsworth's Seat", and, from a lower point, it commands the sunset view the aged poet had from his Rydal Mount above, with the grey-blue Langdale Pikes rising beyond the brown rocks on the nearer horizon.

At the foot of Rydal Water the current gently moves together across a shallow all bearded with water-grass, then begins to rustle down the throat of the pass, with the crags of Nab Scar overhanging the village, and the steeps of Loughrigg Fell crowding from the opposite side. At one time the village "green" of Rydal must have come down to the water's edge, but the church and several cottages now occupy the area. Therefore, to watch the clear stream, you must now pass over to the Loughrigg side. It is a merry brook, perhaps twenty feet wide and less than a foot deep on the bars. It begins to sing as it dances over the rounded stones. The people whose gardens come down to Wordsworth's Rothay should revel in water music: they show their love and delight by edgings and borders of old-fashioned plants which the poet loved, and thereby add scent and colour to the water-side.

In Wordsworth's day the first crossing of the Rothay, in time of flood, was at Pelter Bridge, a single stone arch with a flood culvert next the fields. Below this the river dozes in a long narrow trough which the sunshine dapples with the shadows of alder and sycamore leaves. A stream from Rydal Park now comes to a very beautiful "Meeting of the Waters", after which the combined stream goes quietly across the meadows for half a mile, haunt of dipper and gorgeous kingfisher, and with brakes of figwort and brooklime.

Here come Wordsworth's Stepping-Stones, on a quieter path from Ambleside to Rydal Mount. The laburnum drops golden fountains among the paper white of bird cherry and cream of late hawthorn, and the pastures are mantled in red and white and gold over a surtout of living green. Loughrigg Holme was often visited by Wordsworth, for here Edward Quillinan brought, as his second wife, Dora, the poet's only daughter. "Going to Dora" were the last words the old man said on his deathbed: he was rejoining the daughter who had died a few years before.

Now the stream runs for a mile or so between road and pasture, passing Ambleside in the distance, with Fox Ghyll and Fox Howe, homes of friends of Wordsworth on the Loughrigg slope opposite. Then the deepening Rothay curves away from the hill, runs over another bed of smooth silver shingle, and mingles in the head of the long pool which extends from Rothay Bridge down to the lake. The great poet often came here to meet the swift-striding Christopher North (Professor John Wilson), or the dark-eyed, square-built F. W. Faber, whose devotional verses are so tinged with sadness. Or he might pass here to go to Brathay Bridge, half a mile on the Coniston road, where Charles and Owen Lloyd of Langdale would keep tryst.

Rothay itself has little more story: its banks are lined with flowers, with alders and willows dipping into the smooth streams. Half-way to the lake the Brathay comes in from the west. Ages ago the dalesfolk noticed that in autumn the spawning fish from the lake came into the lowest pool, and then the red-and-gilt char turned into the Brathay, in which there are dark pools and deep wheels, while the silver trout ran up the musical Rothay. Each fish has its own need and instincts.

The combined streams enter the lake alongside a relic of ancient times—the square camp built by the Romans some eighteen centuries ago. One side is guarded by the lake; there is a marsh to the east; and to the west the Rothay has been turned aside to improve a ditch defence. There is not even a sigh as the stream drifts forward into the lake, though it sways beds of water-grass and here and there the red tubes of water-lily stems rising from the muddy floor.

The Poet's Path

In rambling anywhere, but particularly in the Lake Country, an excellent principle decrees that every path should be traversed in both directions. A day or two ago, during a week-end at Grasmere, I recalled this principle, and accordingly traversed the poet Wordsworth's favourite path past Dove Cottage and White Moss tarn, along the front of Nab Scar to Rydal Mount, descending to Rydal village.

The route goes roughly east and west, and I had few recollections of the eastward trip. Indeed, like many other people, I prefer to walk with the sun behind me and not dazzling my eyes. Fate has also decreed that I must arrive at Rydal early in the day, and the choice between that and the path from Pelter Bridge along the Loughrigg side of Rydal Water is obvious.

To me Wordsworth's path has ever a charm; he was an ideal chooser of hill-side ways, a quiet, steady rambler given to introspection and observation rather than to idle talk. He was a knowledgeable man too among the dalesfolk.

Let's tryst this February morning at the corner where the village and Keswick roads part. The hill-tops above 2000 feet are crusted with frozen sleet with here and there a white snowfield, relic of a recent storm. The air is full of sunshine, but the shadows are startlingly chill.

A sign at the lane end indicates Dove Cottage, at which the poet and his sister first settled in Grasmere Vale. Not long before it had held out the sign of the Dove and Olive Branch and offered

> A greeting of good ale
> To all who entered Grasmere Vale.

When Wordsworth arrived, this lane over White Moss was the only access to Grasmere. He was still resident when the new road by

Penny Rock and the lake shore was blasted through, destroying some of his ancient haunts, but taking the increasing traffic away from his cottage door.

> . . . the calmest, fairest spot of earth
> With all its unappropriated good,
> My own.

There are ice-sheets on the rills today, and icicles hang from the water-breaks and mosses. The wind touches shrewdly, and the half-mile climb to White Moss goes easily, but once or twice we turn to look across the lake, across the level fields to Silver How, Helm Crag, and the whitened ridges against the windswept sky beyond.

In a plantation near the little pool where Wordsworth, even in his old age, came for the earliest skating, a woodman has been felling a syca-more and riving the stout branches into staves for fencing. The cart-track past the cottages carries us from the pass to a fine view over Rydalmere with grim Nab Scar on one hand, Loughrigg Fell on the other, and the sunlit Wansfell beyond. The ridge on which stands the poet's home, with its view down two valleys with their lakes, was visible.

Brick red is the dead bracken in the sunshine; the coppice woods are sear and thin, with here and there a green patch of holly, yew or of ivy clinging to some ancient tree. Gorse comes here and there, but there is more of the whippy green rods of the broom, and here and there on the fell is rich evergreen of juniper.

Once entered, Wordsworth's path is obvious, and we shall waste no words on tracing it, mapwise and guide-book fashion. Here and there I look for the bilberry, but February is early for the mantles along the rocky knolls and ledges, for its fresh green verdure. I might point out little devices in fencing and building which have come down the centuries to us—the hogg-holes at the foot of walls for sheep to pass from one enclosure to another; the larger stone, slate-slab, or easily moved obstruction which serves to block them; the stone gate stoops which have holes for bars; the clever dry-stone wall with its double line of "throughs" which bind the structure together in the wildest gale and defy snow and rain.

In February two matters which would have raised the poet's ire are visible: in high summer the bridge which carries the water-pipes from Thirlmere to Manchester is scarcely noticed; while the average tourist does not recognize, in the bracken brae, the "tip" at the entrance to Nab Scar tunnel. Today the alteration of the hill-side is obvious enough; but it is clothed with thin grass and new scree coming from the rocks above, though the lower end of the fan is held up by a superfluous stone wall.

So noting, we have come to the woods, chiefly coppice of hazel (with catkins dangling, half loose, and the red rags of flowers) and oak, with sufficient forest trees to justify the quotation of Dorothy Plowman's lines :

> Perhaps this very woodland here
> Is lovelier than it used to be
> Because some other held it dear,
> And stood and looked from tree to tree,
> And loved it long ago.

The whole hill-side is full of memories of the greatest Nature poet of all.

The foot-path way rises and falls on the grassy hill-side, here and there passing scattered oak, ash or elm trees, with fine views of the rocky islets in the lake below, of great shattered rocks above and a wonderful view of mountain-tops beyond the little lake basin. Then our route rises, and a little gate marks the grounds of Rydal Mount. It marks too the way to Nab Well, the spring from which for 37 years the water-drinking poet's glass was filled at meal-times, and to which he wrote the tribute :

> Mindful that thou (ah! wherefore by my Muse
> So long unthanked) hast cheered a simple board
> With beverage pure as ever fixed the choice
> Of hermit, dubious where to scoop his cell.

Near the gate we halt and look down on the terraced lawns, smooth and comparatively green in an area of rough dead grass. Down there seems to be a flagged expanse with a sundial, a wonderful viewpoint over woods and lake and to the distant hills. On the rib of ground above it appears the poet's summer-house, from which he could look either along Windermere, a glittering scimitar in this February sunshine, or to Rydal Water over which a high floating cloud was casting a blue shadow.

From the little pool of "fringed water-lily" in White Moss to this gate outside the poet's garden, the terrace walk is very lovely all the way, whether you walk through desolation of rock and scree left bare and naked to the sky, or linger in nooks clothed with fern and moss and bracken. With the poet's gate comes the culmination of our ramble, and we take the short track between Rydal Mount and Hart Head Farm, then drop past Rydal Hall gates to the busy road. Today there are some glimpses at first of Windermere through the bare branches, but the flashes soon cease.

Permit me to finish with a question suggested by my opening paragraph : should a rambler travel west or east along Wordsworth's foot-path way beneath Nab Scar? The answer seems easy: take whichever opportunity is offered, whether from Grasmere or Ambleside, and repeat the journey in the opposite direction as soon as you can. Rydal Mount is the home of Wordsworth in his crowned years just as Dove Cottage at the Grasmere end represents the home of his years of unremitting "plain living and high thinking". If your interest is in Wordsworth, the poet and the man, you must proceed from west to east.

The view is quite another question: probably most people would prefer to walk with their faces towards Wetherlam, Crinkle Crags, Bowfell and the Langdale Pikes, with the lake of Rydal below them on the left for half an hour, and the sudden view over Grasmere lake, then village and church, as they drop down the lane to Dove Cottage.

If by this advice I leave you in doubt—do as I have done: travel the foot-path in both directions.

As Skater

William Wordsworth, the greatest of Nature poets, was well known as a first-class skater. The old dalesfolk about Windermere and Rydal used to recall his feat of writing his name with deft strokes and curves on the ice. He was always the first man to be out on skates when the upland tarns or pools began to bear. He would walk from his home at Grasmere up to Easedale tarn or even further for sport.

In his later years he kept up his interest. A small boy was sent ahead to sweep the snow from that "pool, bare to the eyes of Heaven", on White Moss which was frozen days before any other lake or tarn. On his return the wee lad was asked: "What did Mr. Wudswurth do?" He grinned. "I seed him tumm'le." Wordsworth's skate had caught on a stone protruding through the ice-sheet and brought him down with a crash. "He dudn't sweear nor say nowt, but he just sot up and said, 'Eh boy, that was a bad fall, wasn't it?'" Though rather clumsy as a walker, the poet was quite stylish on the ice.

"He would put ya [one] hand i' his breast (he wore a full shirt i' them days), and t'other hand i' his waistband, same as shepherds dea to keep their hands warm, and he would stand up straight and swaay and swing away grandly."

The frozen expanse always attracted Wordsworth; he never forgot his first raptures as a schoolboy on Esthwaite Lake, near Hawkshead, where he had

> Wheeled about,
> Proud and exulting like an untired horse
> That cares not for his home, and shod with steel
> Had hissed along the polished ice.

Thomas de Quincey as 'Statesman

Even to lovers of literary biography, Thomas de Quincey's sole venture as a Westmorland property-owner or 'statesman is practically unknown. Like nearly everything else in the career of that erratic genius it ended in financial disaster. De Quincey came into residence at Dove Cottage, Grasmere—the home for nine years previously of William Wordsworth—in 1809, and eight years later he married Margaret Simpson, daughter of a yeoman living at The Nab, a farm on the shore of Rydal Water.

In 1829 he bought The Nab estate, but it was a phantom ownership, as he had no money, and the estate was again offered for sale in 1833 after De Quincey had settled at Edinburgh. There had been trouble over The Nab property. Old William Park, grandfather of Margaret Simpson, had died, leaving the place burdened with law costs in resisting some feudal fines exacted by his manorial lord. Simpson, who had succeeded by virtue of his wife, applied to De Quincey, for the writer was still regarded as a man of money though his capital had almost disappeared. It was agreed that the writer should buy the estate (which was burdened with a mortgage of £500), giving nominally £2500 for it. De Quincey, who was then in Edinburgh, agreed, and applied to some Manchester solicitors to loan £1400, offering security for the same in the estate.

The firm naturally proceeded with caution; insisted on valuations, and inquired into the validity of John Simpson's claim to the estate through his wife. The steward of the manor said he himself would not give £1000 for all Simpson's land within Rydal; and even with the freehold land outside, its worth was not double that amount.

Yet he admitted that high prices were being paid for land in the Rydal manor:

> The other day Wordsworth the poet purchased a piece of rock (subject to all the inconveniences of customary tenure) at a price almost equal to what is given in large towns for building-ground.

This would be the Rashfield, for which Wordsworth had lately given £300, fearing that he might be turned out of Rydal Mount. The steward goes on:

> De Quincey is a gentleman and Simpson, his father-in-law, is a sober, regular man—rather too much influenced by his Wife to litigation, but I believe he is now sick of it.

The Manchester lawyers next objected to the abstract of title—not comprehending that these lands were held not by deed but by witness of the community at the village court.

In his correspondence, De Quincey (who, by the way, still signed "Thomas Quincey" and wrote from 18 Pitt Street, Edinburgh) lauds the character of the Westmorland estatesmen, but with regard to the abstract he added:

> I fear, from the knowledge I have of the carelessness in this particular prevalent among Westmorland 'statesmen, and from the imperfect legal assistance which they resorted to until very lately (often no better than the parish clerk, sexton, schoolmaster, &c.), that so far the defect will be found to be irremediable.

The £1400 asked for was raised, but the lawyers took the precaution of transferring the estate not to De Quincey direct, but to the man who forwarded the documents.

Before the transaction was complete there was a serious crisis: John Simpson had to meet an execution taken out for the lawsuit expenses, and had to find £250 at once. Mrs. Simpson, in whose right he held The Nab, became seriously ill and there was a fear that she might die, in which case the deal would be ended. However, the money came in due time; the elder Simpson's debts were paid off, and De Quincey found himself with £500 in his hands. At once all was peace and joy, and De Quincey took at least temporary possession, for in 1829 he invited Knight to come down with his wife:

> And now, my friend, think what a glorious Eldorado of milk and butter, and cream-cheeses, and other dairy products, supposing that you like those things, I can offer you morning, noon, and night. You may absolutely bathe in new milk, and even in cream; and you *shall* bathe, if you like it. . . . I could offer (other) temptations—mountain lamb equal to Welsh; char famous to the antipodes; trout and pike from the very lake within twenty-five feet of our door.

Settled as a 'statesman, De Quincey sent his boys to a school at Rydal, and one has talked to several who were educated alongside them. One Grasmere man remembered having once seen the Opium Eater himself. Then the family removed permanently to Edinburgh in 1831, though the tenancy of Dove Cottage (really on account of his tons of books) did not end until 1834, a period of 25 years.

De Quincey's estate venture soon came to an end. For two years the interest was unpaid, and finally the writer's mother paid up £140 plus £40 for lawyers' fees. In acknowledging the amount the Manchester lawyers said:

For the present we will not proceed to sell the estate at Rydal we trust however that the future int: will be regularly paid half yearly by Mr. Quincey—if it is not our client will assuredly exercise his power of sale unless, which we would much prefer, Mr. Quincey can find some one who will take a transfer of the security.

The case was hopeless ; interest was not met, and a year later The Nab estate was advertised for sale, at the Salutation Inn, Ambleside, in September 1833. After this the little estate, possessed by the Park family from time immemorial, passed to the Rydal manor, and the 'statesman with his family and personal belongings left the old home for ever.

John Simpson himself sought refuge with the De Quinceys at Edinburgh.

Westmorland and Hogarth

Westmorland is proud of its connection with Hogarth, the satirical painter, whose fore-elders were born in the county. Richard Hoggart, father of the painter, was the second son, and was sent to St. Bees Grammar School for education. Afterwards he went to London as a schoolmaster and married a City wife, who softened the old name by dropping a g and adding an h. John, the eldest son, succeeded to the family acres. Thomas, the third, was Bohemian in his outlook, and became "Auld Hoggart the Rhymester".

Thomas was married, and died in 1710, having, by marriage or industry, acquired a little property. It is not always safe to take a rhymester at his own account, but Thomas's *Taming of the Shrew* begins with :

> The song which I intend to sing, touch women most of all,
> Yet loath I am that any here should with me scold and brawl,
> For I've enough of that, at home, at home, and eke in bed,
> And once for singing of this song my wife she broke my head.

According to the long, long song, an over-mettlesome wife was first buried in a dark hay-mow ; then tied and blood drawn from under her tongue. She still remained a scold until her husband "took a pair of pincers strong, and a large tooth pulled out", and threatened to draw another if she misbehaved again.

> And from that day until her death, she proved a loving wife;
> Kind, humble, and obedient still, and so did end their strife.

In Troutbeck his cottage had a carved cupboard fixed in the wall

EVENING SPLENDOUR AMONG THE HIGH FELLS, LANGDALE PIKES
IN DISTANCE

"WINTER FRIEZE", SKATING AT WORDSWORTH'S RYDALMERE

bearing the inscription $\frac{T}{A}$ H, 1693, also another marked GH 1710, and an armchair GH 1697 was kept in the dale, having been purchased at a sale of the Hogarth property. No branch of the family, however, has lived in Troutbeck for the last century or so.

Auld Hoggart was often in trouble by his songs, and legend says that he had one eye knocked out by the stick of a dalesman who resented his familiar allusions. After that, the rhymester always ascertained who was in the ale-house company before he began to sing.

He was both dramatist and actor. One of his plays, *The Destruction of Troy*, was given at Troutbeck years after his death. Adam Walker, the dales lad who became London's most popular scientific lecturer, took part in this, and has left a description. The play took place in the open, and "there were more spectators for three days together, than your three theatres in London would hold". Eighty-one years ago Auld Hoggart's *Remnants of Rhyme* were printed from a bundle of MS. which "contained an enormous mass of poetry in the handwriting of Thomas Hoggart, and chiefly of his own composition". Probably the *Remnants* exhibit none of the higher qualities of poetry. The bundle from which they were extracted does not seem to be available, so whether Thomas was poet as well as rhymester in the lines which castigated his neighbours cannot be proved.

CHAPTER FOUR

CYCLING YARNS

Seeing Wild Life—Heron of Dunmail Raise—Riders in the Rain—Cycle Alone for Fun—Girdling the Lake Country.

OF all travellers the cyclist should see most of wild nature. He can progress with the minimum of sound and, by using his brakes, can silently stop to observe anything which comes in his range of vision. In many rides I have had fair fortune in seeing "sporting creatures". The long-legged hares are on the move, and may be seen cantering along the grassy wayside. At full speed they may travel awhile at 35 miles per hour, and are outside the racing of any but exceptional riders. When one presses the hare to a race, it leads gallantly, and then makes a swift side-wise leap; in a few bounds it is

D

over the wall or through the fence or hedgerow. In districts where
game is abundant, the keepers net every hare once, and give it such a
dread of the poacher's device which is hung on gateways that the
creature prefers to leap stiff fence or ditch rather than pass through the
ordinary bars.

Rabbits are seen outside their coverts by quiet riders; bold old
fellows take no notice of passing pedallars, but they are wonderfully
acute to the action of brakes. Before one's toe trails on the ground,
they are up and away for cover. The timid does and youngsters may
have two or three jumps start, but the rotund father-bunnies catch up
and pass them in a terrific burst.

The fox varies in manners from the skulker which glides across the
road in a sinister dusk to the gentleman who trots along, intent on his
business at the farm or poultry-field. It is surprising how well he
carries out the deception that he is a slim sort of dog: the odd cyclist
who detects the imposture, however, has no time for action, as Rey-
nard at once detects danger and springs away. A year or two ago I
drew attention to a little creature creeping out of some bushes and
gradually nearing some hens. In the next field a tumultuous village
cup-tie was being played, and yet the fox nipped its bird, ran across
the road and disappeared in the woods. The first cyclist saw the tag
of a disappearing tail, and that was all.

Of game birds, not a little is seen from the saddle. The gorgeous
and lordly pheasant knows himself to be a superior type of poultry,
and displays his fine feathers, aristocratic steps, and idiotic manners
just within the gamekeeper's paradise. Sometimes one may swing
round a quiet corner of the woodland lane and find this king cleaning
his plumage in a dust-bath of a rut. A multi-coloured rocket streaks
up into the sky, with an explosive "chor-awk" like the muffled cry of a
child who has fallen headlong into deep water. The partridge has
less to do with cycleable roads, though more than once, in extremely
quiet country, I have found a family party still asleep. The birds lie
out in the open, far away from tufts which might shelter a fox, and
make a perfect shield, with tails towards the centre and heads out in
every direction. Only the swift, silent cyclist has the slightest chance of
human approach, and his vision of the sleeping party is brief. The
birds burst off in all directions with a wonderful rattling of wings.

For grouse you must ride the green roads of the high moors; if
you travel early, soon after light is spreading across the heather and
grass, the birds are feeding and are comparatively slow to take wing.
On a warm noon they are more alert: one sees a red eyepatch above
the heather, and then the bird is off, with a rush of wings and then a
volplane on stiff pinions around the corner of the hill and out of sight.

Occasionally one disturbs the sentry of a covey or a family, a bird which goes off the rock or peat-hag with a defiant crow, and then the others whirl up from all sides and are away before the cyclist—or other evil trespasser—has any chance of doing mischief.

Occasionally one may disturb the handsome mallard or wild duck, or the wee teal, as the machine sweeps down some slope, and of course moorhens are fairly regularly seen, trotting back, with many a complaint and dive for some insect or other trifle, over the bosky grass towards the thicket next the pool or river. My most startling occurrence was the sudden crash of a tall heron from a marsh dyke sunk between road and wood. The grey face, white beard with dark spots, the silver-tipped wings, the golden-red eye with its black streak and rim, were quite plain as I came up. The bird tumbled over a great mass of heather, screamed with wild terror, and hit the top of a willow bush before its nerves were under command and it could take a flight line for the clear air.

In Scotland I have seen, in spring, as the miles passed beneath the wheels, a pair of golden eagles flying high or swinging round some great cliff, but more impressive was an evening scene, on Shap Fell, in Westmorland. I had come south for miles through soft showers, and there was mist of the last one still creeping across the moor. Then as the road curved over the ridge towards Wasdale Bridge, the moist clouds split, and through a narrow gate came golden sunshine. And in the ray of glory, with the light touching its wings, hung a great buzzard, big as a minor eagle. In a few seconds the clouds pushed together, the moor was drenched with a soft shower, and mist quenched the last sight of the great bird curving about like a moth in the distance.

Any cyclist who uses his machine aright is privileged by many a glimpse into wild nature. I have found a young cuckoo on the grass, because its foster parents, the meadow pipits, made such a darting and tumult. And one day a mother weasel with eight whelps in a pack behind her trotted down the road. I did not ride over the party as I might have tried to do, but passed by—on the other side. My ankles spun all the more gladly when I noticed the lady's evil little face and flashing teeth turned towards me. Despite country legends, I am still loth to believe that any of our larger stoats, let alone the tiny weasel, which is merely the thickness of a round desk-ruler, willingly attacks any human being. Yet a mother in defence of her young will attempt the improbable, the impossible.

The quiet cyclist can see much more than the miles of road, forest shadows, and sweeping vistas of country if he chooses to turn an eye towards wild nature, the ever present, the undisturbed and yet inscrutable.

Heron of Dunmail Raise

"After it, get along." But the top speed of a cycle through the trough of Dunmail Raise is too slow to catch up with a heron flying high above. For half a mile the grey bird was kept more or less in sight, then it rose higher and higher until it was a mere wisp in the sky and, as it turned towards Helvellyn, the bird was lost to view.

The heron had been disturbed from a pool beneath some rowans on the Grasmere side of the pass, and was well on the wing before I noticed it.

Often I have watched birds migrate through this gap of Dunmail Raise. In February I have stood on the road and listened, in the darkness, to the wings and calls of the geese going north; in March and April first come the house-martins, then the swallows, and finally the big black swifts. They pass every minute from dawn to dusk, and one has no proof that they do not travel by night as well.

As the heron flew steadily away over the deep trench in the hills, one could not help thinking of the old times when its tribe was a royal dish; when they were preserved for hawking. Rare enough is there a present-day record of a heron being attacked by a falcon. Once at any rate a heron with broken neck was found on the fells above a marshy wood. The keeper believed that this was proof that a peregrine had struck it. This fierce hawk strikes down wood-pigeons, rock-doves and even homers for very mischief, going through a flock dealing death right and left and never dropping to see what has happened to the dead bodies. From the rocks above St. Bee's Head one has seen this wilful work carried out among puffins and razorbills as well as gulls. There's little chance of escape when the little red hawk settles seriously to pursuit. Its speed and ferocity are beyond words; the mile-a-minute pigeon certainly has no chance in comparison.

Though apparently slow in its wing-beats, the heron still gets away at a respectable pace. At first I could see the strong beak resting on the breast, the grey sweep of pinions, and the long legs trailing behind, but our speed was too slow and the bird gradually rose up and away.

I wonder how far a heron can see; certainly the birds keep to definite tracks in their flights. On the shore of Thirlmere is a tree on which they roost; a single pine standing out on a headland near a deep gorge. The dales folk sometimes note the time at which Jammie passes to each bog and river-pool, where they fish for frogs or small trout. "Mother, the Jammie is at the bottom of the field again; it's time for the postie to come, isn't it?" This was actually heard in the Legburthwaite valley.

Riders in the Rain

"It is better riding in the rain."

How often is that boast of the well-equipped veteran heard when the club, already delayed by evil weather, faces the possibility of a stormy return by the longest road home. But for it the party would save time by taking a shorter round.

The veteran may really relish a ride through the rain because there is waiting for him sure comfort, dry clothes, a hot bath, a warm meal; no black looks or querulous criticism. It is easy to ride to a welcome, but many of the club party may have at the back of their minds an equal certainty of trouble. Their equipment is by no means so thorough, and wet feet and stockings are pretty sure to come.

"If he rides through, so shall we," say the youths of the wheel— and they face the music from hostile landladies and sometimes parents as well.

The veteran should remember that his words and actions are taken as a challenge, and the lads wish to prove that they are not less hardy than he is. But they may not take home pools of mud and rivers of rainwater with impunity, as he does. Only a part of the battle is fought out on the road.

Many lads who are working away from home (and these form the bulk of winter riders) find that traces of road sport are looked at askance in rooms and lodgings. After an evening run, the room is cold, fires not properly lit, and not even the possibility of a warm wash. While not willing to "kill the goose that lays the golden eggs" (i.e. the lodgers), a good deal of awkwardness can be indulged when the rider comes home, drenched to the skin and mud-stained because his all-weather equipment is less complete than that of the veteran.

There is admittedly pleasure in pedalling, behind a good lamp, on a dark and rainy night. But the cyclist must have thorough equipment, and be willing to journey at a moderate speed. A club in which the leader knows that several riders are badly equipped is apt to try fast paces, and the end is not a gain but a loss. The man at the rear of the party has to signal through the motor-cars which catch up. Many drivers, despite the help of screen-wipers, feel that their outlook is impaired during rain, and travel at slow speeds. I have known a club to keep in front of the headlights of such a car for a mile or two—

and the wavings of the beams among feet and tyres were rather amusing. Indeed the car was a help rather than a hindrance, for its lights showed the road far in front, and gave the leader a shine to himself at the corners.

When riding through the rain, the cyclist should keep an open mind about other users of the road. Usually, if room is given, they will go past the club with the minimum amount of mud-splashing from the wheels. Indeed, the car which travels at a moderate speed is a better friend than that other which sweeps wide and sends up plumes of mud and water from the far side of the crown. The pedestrian complains that after the passage of a score of cycles his clothes are spattered with wet and mud just as though a car had gone by at high speed. Sometimes he or she is right.

Regular speed and even pedalling in the rain reduces the risk of a skid. All the same, the leader should be given a little more start than usual for he is the first to come across greasy paths, belts of leaves, and the like. The trembling of his back tyre is warning for his followers. The pairs, and even the rearguard, should put an extra length between. In my experience of club runs, I think the damage is mainly to the machine that skids, and rarely is there a mix-up involving several riders and their mounts.

This is a tribute to the better discipline and wariness of regular riders. On a slippery day, where town traffic is stopped by robots or traffic-constables, it is not unusual to come across two or three messenger-boys and such wild riders who have had a spill involving the whole party. I agree that these lads take appalling risks at times, but their very unconcern disarms criticism.

To return to our original point—"It is better to ride in the rain," says the veteran—what can a club leader do in the matter?

I am inclined to look upon him as a sort of trustee, as a rider who will see that the club's full programme is carried through, but on a wet night, when he knows that many of the party are occupiers of rooms and lodgings, it is within his province either to split the men who are assured of a welcome home from the ordinary riders, or to give orders for a short run back to the town, a run in which there will be the minimum of mud-splattering and rain-soaking.

I am quite aware that this outlook is open to criticism, but there is a point at which a club leader is entitled to ask whether his followers into the rain are likely to suffer after the ride. He can indicate a fresh route, or split the party. Youngsters in their first lodgings should never be permitted to go on, half-equipped as they usually are against the storm, because they believe that their skill or hardiness is questioned or challenged.

Most leaders, especially those who come out with the smaller winter parties, are easily able to pick out those who are likely to have a cooler reception on their return than the veterans, married or otherwise, who have settled homes. The first experience of hostility, veiled or open, against a young cyclist in rooms or lodgings is a pretty bad experience, and that an "all-weather career" is risked. Already far too many youngsters have bidden farewell to their club friends, dismantled and cleaned their cycles for winter, and they will not appear on the road again until after Easter of next year. Some of these may turn up for the winter dances and socials promoted by wise committees who desire to keep their members together, but a lot drift away from the sport altogether, and do not resume with the next season.

Cycle Alone For Fun

Cycle the road alone for fun—that's a good motto. Frederick the Great used to say that a council of war meant the acceptance of the view of the chicken-hearted among warriors. It is true that the mere presence of a companion, however complacent, makes one think ahead and so the adventures do not come. North, south, east, and west—my winter trips in company never have any zest or mustard, never any fun of the grim sardonic sort. From an old ragamuffin loafing through the gloaming on Shap Fell I learnt the latest code of tramp signals—the house to avoid, the dangerous dog, the "easy mark" where a good tale always brings a bit of silver. "Mighty few of them places since the Lloyd George came in : there's no loose money kept on the kitchen shelf for the poor tramps, and mighty little spare grub either." We chatted awhile, then he cheerfully suggested :

"It's getting dark—what prevents me trying to bash you ?"

The place was certainly lonesome, but I had no intention of allowing a "stand or deliver" trick.

"Only the certainty that you would get a good hammering if you tried," was my reply.

"Good enough," was the cheery rejoinder. He meant no harm, as he said, so hoped that there was no offence. Now, would he have suggested such a thing to two cyclists ? I think not. We parted friends—of a sort, but he was no richer. I'm not a George Borrow : I do not share his love for ale nor his hatred of ruined abbeys and Jesuits, but somehow, without much effort, I have picked up a few words of real lore of the road. George Borrow, by the way, loved to roam and romance alone : witness the mushy conventionality of *Wild Wales*, where the author's wife and adopted daughter were on hand to check his first story with the second, and the wild exuberance of *Lavengro* when he travelled as a solitary bachelor. It wasn't that George was an older or wiser fellow in the Welsh times, but that he was better watched in regard to his stories.

Years ago I used to meet a tramp on a noisy old solid-tyred cycle; he abandoned the machine when a friend of the road who had borrowed it for a nine-mile spin walked the route back and declined, with most regrettable emphasis, to either ride or push the offensive vehicle. "It's worse than hard labour is that treadmill." And surely Gipsy John was the man to know. Sometime afterward old Sammy appeared without his machine. "I'm getting on in years now, and folk think that, when I ride a bike, I'm too healthy to get anything without a lot of hard work. It was a terrible heavy thing to pedal." And certainly with all the tramps' gear hanging and banging over frame and handle-bars, it was a fully-loaded affair.

North Country, Scottish, and Welsh roads and tracks have pro-vided most of one's winter adventures, but one has travelled southern miles as well. Compared with the northern moors and passes, even the wildest of southern roads seem easy; their pitches may be abrupt, but most of them are short and their tricks obvious. Yet one may happen on adventure, when and where it is least expected. A hys-terical dame hurled fearful language—and a rolling-pin—at me because one asked her wan, terrified youngster the way. "I telled him that I wouldn't have him talk with strangers." I pitied the child, but retreat was the best policy, at least out of range of her missiles. After a while her screams and words ceased, and she called the child in for tea in quite a different tone of voice.

"And as for you, if there was a policeman here, I'd make him take you up. Standing there, just waiting your chance to entice an innocent child away from its mother—yes, you'd better be off."

As peace seemed to be declared in the home, I mounted and quietly pedalled away.

Winter rides in the West Country seem to be famous for head-winds. "Yes," said the Devon farmer, "it would be better to train to Penzance and let the wind blow you back, except that it's varying a bit now, and by morning might be a gale blowing you on over Land's End." And so it was. However, my route had changed to due south, along the coast, and the cross-wind being stronger was almost as bad as the head breeze had been. Yet on that day the cycle brought me to a nook where the road slipped half-way down the cliff, and gave me the vista of a most appalling cross-sea. For miles extended a jostle of broken water, in which any small craft would be in great peril. One felt glad that cycling kept to hard roads and not to wet and tumbling seas.

As I had recently seen a fight between wind and tide in the Pentland Firth, off the north of Scotland, there was a parallel to recall. The northern battle was fought under a leaden pall, but here the light was comparatively sunshine, a wan silver gleam with blue sky overhead. "It's safer here than out there today," said the old roadman, waving his hammer towards the turmoil. "I always work hereabout in winter, for this nook is sheltered from most winds, and I like to see the storm out at sea."

I have reason to remember that day, for just at dusk a great windblast romped across the road from a totally unexpected angle, and shook cycle and man to such effect that my ride ended in a stout and prickly tangle of brambles. The thorns engaged my attention for some time until suddenly the darkness fell around. Nor was that the end of misadventure. I had been told of a village with a goodly inn, but the place eluded me, and up and down steep lanes and along the edge of a moor I sought in vain. A flash of moonlight through hurrying clouds gave vision of a village church, but it was far away in the eye of the wind, and when reached proved to be a lonely fane at an unmarked cross-roads. In desperation I chose the descending route, and for five miles there was incline—and at the end an empty beach where later I was told an occasional ferry-boat plied to some fishing-hamlets bunched in a cove a mile away. So back through the silent glen, now fighting every yard against wind and slope, and hoping to meet some wayfarers. A ploughman was standing at the cross-roads by the church. "Inn?—why, it's just over the rise not two minutes away. . . . Yes, I know there's a road up the moor, but the inn's at the bottom of the hill. . . . What a pity you rode down to the old ferry-beach. . . . There's three roads through those woods, and you passed the end of every one on 'em, and they would have brought you to houses. Didn't you see any roads at all? Well, well."

In the south country, one has ordinary quarters in winter—sometimes a room damp with moorland mist, sometimes touched with sea spray, sometimes with a few bronze-winged butterflies which have flown to the shelter beneath the thatch for winter. One finds sometimes that the builder who inserted a big green glass-sheet in the wall facing sea or moor was a wise man after all. Otherwise the moisture couldn't fail to drive through into the rooms. Once a bungalow high up the cliff was shown me as a pretty sleeping-place, but the lady demurred: "In winter we can only sleep in the back rooms; the spray from the rocks drifts right through the casements into the others."

On a Wiltshire lane, the cottager who came out of the house reckoned that "you must be hungry, mister, but we've nothing worthy

to offer you." He carried my cycle across two fields, and placed me on
the direct road to a town, exactly where has long been forgotten.
Sometimes, in recalling old times and roads, I wish that my cycle experiences had come in the pioneer days when curious mistakes were made.
"Hi, John," shouted the dame to her husband, "doan't ee go out yet.
That scissors-grinder fellow has just gone mad; he's treadling his
wheel all over the road."

Looking around the dinner-table where a number of veteran
cyclists sat, one recalled another story which was hailed as familiar.
"No cyclists here," said the maid of the inn; "you see, we reckons to
keep respectable company." Some of the old squires and farmers,
and even parsons, were bitter against all wheelers, and one night, at a
log fire in the New Forest, the following was heard:

"And pa'son, he says from the pulpit right out, 'If the Lord God
had intended men to roll about the road, then He would have provided
the wheels.'"

Then the lads began to argue whether that was the Sunday when
pa'son preached down the cyclists, or merely alluded to the Saturday-
night custom of several villagers who found two legs inadequate for the
journey home from the inn. Finally, it seemed to be decided that the
cycling sermon had something about the fiery, sulphury pit and that
he had never said *that* about the local pot-wallopers. "But you
needn't mind that, mister." Now what did that lad really mean?
I preferred to pay for the obvious drink rather than inquire further.

Only in Sussex and highest Cornwall did we find inns of the solid
Northern sort, defying the wildest gale, and with their thick walls
reducing the roar to a mere rumble heard at intervals when the talk
round the fireside made pause. One found the people inclined to
accept as gospel the most grisly were-wolf yarns rather than the
common run of ghost stories, and always ready to marvel at the
daring of the man who rode alone in winter, and apparently cared but
little for storm and dusk. "Don't ee shiver sometimes in the strange
wild places?"

In these days winter riders are by no means rare even in furthest
England. We come into our own when the motorists leave the road.
"'Tis a strange way of seeking amusement," but it's an excellent way
too. Cycle alone for fun, but avoid the ladies, please. A youth,
fired to emulation by a haphazard but truthful yarn of mine, insinu-
ated himself into the family circle at a Somerset inn, and took part in
a dance held in an upper room. He found that a few heedless invita-
tions to the ladies as partners made him unpopular with the supplanted
local youth, and at one crisis it looked as though he might have to fight
a whole gang. However, he dodged the conflict, retired from the

dance for supper, and went to bed. He asked my opinion on his return :
What should I have done ? And one remembered very well a practically identical incident. But then—I had kissed each of the ladies
under the mistletoe ! Enough to cost a few blows. I did wish for a
friendly fist or two that night.

Cycle alone—and no one can correct or refute the impressions which
may vary with the company ; nor can one be caught out when side-
stepping the truth in answering some question. If I had admitted, in a
bar or inn, that the tour was to furnish material for the pen of a
writer, the whole pose would be changed. I prefer to hear natural
talk, songs, jokes, and stories all the time. My work with the pen is
not an obsession when travel is astir ; the impressions can wait until
there is reason to write a long letter home. And once a winter revel
in the Cotswolds was recorded alongside a shorthand note of a speech
made by mine host of the inn to his guests. It was a funny affair,
really, but too long to begin here.

Girdling the Lake Country

When the road-maps come down on the table, my wife protests :
"There you go—putting folks up to rides you don't go yourself."
The objection is sound : it's easier to plan than to carry out a continuous girdle of the Lake Country. I've done it all, in winter and in
summer, but never at a continuous trip. The job can be done in a
long week-end or it can cover the longest Christmas holiday, just as
the cyclist prefers to mix other things with hard riding on the roads.

Kendal is the starting-point from the south, but the cyclist can
pick up the girdle-route at Keswick from the north, or at Penrith from
the east. The crossing of many passes is involved in the route, so
machine and kit should suit the task. Brakes should be in good order.
The awkward descents on the hills can be easily noticed from
above, and as a rule they are very short. A couple of hundred yards
on foot makes a mighty difference on a double-corner. But there
are long inclines and head-winds which need the help of a low gear.

The first sector should be direct from Kendal to the Ferry across
Windermere, then by Sawrey and Hawkshead to Coniston. This
is all fair road, hilly, with some motor-buses at first, but afterwards
quite open going. There are marvellous views of the fells and lakes
as one travels along. At Coniston you must decide whether you will
take your cycle for a walking tour over Walna Scar pass, a track which
rises to 2035 feet, to Seathwaite in the Duddon valley. It's hard
pedestrian graft all the way, and your kit does not make for comfort-

able pushing. The path, however, is not too bad—the worst surface is the pitch beyond the railway bridge at Coniston which is kept in a ploughed condition by the descending slate-carriers. Still, there is wet and mud and stony going at parts, and the descent to the Duddon is steep. The rider can also go west through Torver and reach sea-level at Duddon Bridge without actually touching Broughton-in-Furness, or he can turn off for Broughton Mills and push over the steep ridge to Dunnerdale, about a mile from Seathwaite. Probably in either case he will aim at the old inn near the

Kirk of Ulpha,
To the pilgrim's eye, as welcome as a star.

From Duddon Bridge to Ulpha there is a steep climb of maybe a mile, after which the road undulates down to Ulpha, with a decided trend to free-wheeling all the way. Between Seathwaite and Ulpha the lanes are tortuous, with plenty of little hills but no great gain in height.

If an early start is made from Kendal, the first day might include a run alongside Coniston Water, passing Brantwood, where John Ruskin lived for so many years. Go into Coniston village first, then return to the waterhead, and, after rounding the foot of the lake six miles away, turn back for Torver. There are shorter but not easier and certainly not finer routes for the cyclist between Lowick Green and Duddon Bridge.

For rough riding from Ulpha, take the lane to Seathwaite and the deteriorating track towards Cockley Beck. Here a turn into the steep Hard Knott pass takes one over to Eskdale. It's no place for a cyclist in wintry weather, and the Roman Camp up there must have been a perishing outpost. Legend says that the place was occupied as a strafe camp for soldiers. It's a cold, windy place.

It is better to proceed up the steep Ulpha bank above the Ulpha Inn to Birker moor, where there is a bit of riding before one tumbles over the edge to Dalegarth Force in Eskdale. Try a ride up this valley : if there are no floods, the going's easy, and the machine can be taken beyond Butterelkeld into a wonderful "cirque" of rock peaks. The great buttresses and soaring ridges of Bowfell, Great End, Esk Pike, Scafell Pike and Scafell (probably topped and seamed with snow) make a fine sight.

The retreat is down the dale to Eskdale Green, then over the moor to Irton and Santon Bridge, where there is a hilly road to Wast-water. A good rider will conquer all the inclines, but to others a few are stiff. It's no disgrace to walk up the few score yards necessary after a stiff pull. Hill-climbing on a cycle needs skill and careful use of power rather than brute strength. There's no cycle route forward from Wasdale Head: if there's ice and snow about, it's unwise to trying shoving over to Borrowdale. Cycling-shoes do not give the best grip on loose stones, bog-moss, ice or snow. Return by the side of Wastwater, taking the road to Seascale at the finest viewpoint of this amazing lake, and at Gosforth turn along the Whitehaven road to Calder Bridge. Here a mountain-road, quite suitable for riding where it is not too steep, goes to Ennerdale Bridge, and one might end the day's work at the Anglers' Inn, on the shore of the lake. This is, however, a big place nowadays and not so cheap as one remembers the old one to have been. There are quarters, homely but sufficient, at Ennerdale Bridge.

Ennerdale also has no through-route for the pedaller, and indeed one doesn't recommend travel beyond the Anglers' Inn, though there is a rough cart-track to Gillerthwaite and even into the "forest" beyond. The Pillar Rock, as seen from the lake, forms part of a very striking bit of mountain scenery with the dark lake as foreground. From Ennerdale, the road passes through Lamplugh to a wide stretch of moorland whence one can look across the Solway to Criffel and the peaks of Dumfrieshire and Galloway. The country below lies spread out like a map with the great blue inlet lying, like a sword, between the countries of England and Scotland. By the way, an early-day view of the Isle of Man from the West Cumberland moors is regarded as a symptom of wild weather approaching; the sunset view is not a weather portent at all.

The descent of Fangs Brow to Loweswater is pretty steep, but this out-of-the-way lake is very interesting. Over the next ridge lies Crummock Water, and one pedals alongside the whole eastern shore, sometimes on a shelf which seems almost to overhang the water. There is one corner which is quite exciting as the road creeps round a great crag and gives a sudden glimpse of the distant fells. At Buttermere, the next point, one prefers to recommend escape to Keswick over Newlands Hause. The up-climb is severe, but it is road, and once the zigzags on the Newlands side are descended there is free-wheeling for miles, ending with a nasty "Devil's Elbow" just beyond Newlands Hotel. Beyond this the road has no difficulty to Keswick. If the day is young, with a couple of hours of good light, Honister pass can be tackled. The ride up the Buttermere road is easy, and so is the turn into the cove beneath Honister pass. However, when the pass does decide to rise, there is stiff pushing indeed for a short distance which seems to be long. The upper sector is usually running with water in winter. A strong and patient person will win through, but anybody less blessed will be sorry. In any case, it is not difficult to make retreat to Buttermere, and reach Keswick by a longer and easier route. Over the pass there is a long descent, with some bad pitches down to Seatollar, where the level is reached. This is about seven miles from Keswick. Accommodation, however, can be obtained "on the spot", or at Rosthwaite. Some of the hotels hereabout are partially closed in winter, but distances and roads alike are easy to the cyclist.

From Keswick our girdle-route goes on by Threlkeld to Trout-beck, passing under the very screes of Saddleback, and then crossing the wild Matterdale Common to Ullswater, but the winter student of Lake Country beauty is advised to make for Grasmere by Thirlmere and Dunmail Raise. This is a civilized route, with motor-buses run-ning all the winter, and not deserted as it used to be. Ambleside, at the end of this sector, is at the foot of an excessively steep struggle to Kirkstone pass. The little inn is often buried in mist for a week in winter, and when there are even wisps of cloud astir it is foolish to ride down any of the long grades to Patterdale. Kirkstone is a gate-way to Ullswater, and is worth a bit of trouble. This is, however, confined to the two steep bits about Ambleside and below the summit inn (with a mile of riding in between), and another corner just at the steepest bit of the descent.

The last section is from Ullswater by Shap Fell to Kendal, and the exact route depends upon time and light and weather, the last most of all. Personally one would prefer to round off the list of lakes visited by turning from Pooley Bridge through the lakes to Askham, with a view of Lowther Castle on the way, then through Helton to Bampton. Near the latter a road goes off into the fells, coming to a dead end at the head of Haweswater.

You must return to Bampton, unless the steep rough pass of Gatescarth to Longsleddale is tackled. In winter this is often covered with ice and snow and is not a place to recommend. From Bampton to Shap there is a big hill, and after that fair running for the remaining miles. The road south (A6) from Shap has often been described. Coming in this way the climb is less severe, for Shap itself is 900 feet up on the way to the 1304 feet of the summit some six miles away. The descent to Kendal goes in easy sweeps and the hill at High Borrow Bridge is the only one to relieve the miles of easy going.

Such a girdle-route is worth the while of any adventurous youth or pair of youths. There is plenty of collar work and a lot to see which is hidden from the summer tourist. There is colour in the woods, by the lakes and along the hill-sides, while the mountains may be capped with snow and great rocks masked with ice. There may be gales and rain, and there may be days so clear that your breath is taken away by the sudden revelations of beauty. But that is a topic one must not touch lest enthusiasm outstrip discretion. No one can promise clear sky in winter, and the moist air near the sea often gives haze which is most irritating to the traveller.

The road-passes for the most part are not difficult, but when snow and ice are astir the utmost vigilance and caution are needed. In riding over a crust of snow, on level roads, a steady pace and even pedalling is necessary, and steering must be careful rather than sudden. A swing of the body usually means that the machine broadsides and leaves one rolling on the snow. Ice is a problem which one does not tackle on rubber tyres; usually the condition is temporary in time and small in area. It is rare that the Lake Country passes are snow-covered for more than a day or two, but if one is snowbound the pleasures may be greater. Borrowdale with hoar or snow on its birches is one of the loveliest sights the world can show.

CHAPTER FIVE

SEEN THROUGH MY TENT DOOR

Flower Time—Mud—Moths—Friends: Cattle and Sheep—Buttermere in
       Storm.

'Tis like the birthday of the world,
When earth was born in bloom;
The light is made of many dyes,
The air is all perfume;
There's crimson buds, and white and blue,
The very rainbow showers
Have turned to blossoms where they fell,
And sown the earth with flowers.

WHO can write like Tom Hood? Yet May has its message for everyone who will come out to the fields and woods and take notice. From my tent-door I look across a cream glory of hawthorn spread over the hedgerows; over dry banks all covered with cowslips with delicate spotted throats. Golden king-cups or marsh marigolds sprawl in lazy beauty round every drain-mouth and spring; the lady's smock is a fabric of lilac shimmering over the fresh green grass.

The world is very full of flowers today. The tall larch has quaint rosy tufts on its highest branches; the horse-chestnut is beginning to light its myriad candles of crimson and white; the sycamore is strewing its waste of green yellow in the grass, for the clusters come early. The hornbeam shows untidy yellowish flowers, and the wayfaring tree, another semi-alien to our north country, has its mealy-looking leaves and crowded white flowers. The oak has ceased to show red bud-tips, and is ready to burst into green leaves; already there are some little green threads which are part of its flowering activities.

In every damp nook there seems to be a clump of red-robin, a ragged chap who never seems to be other than old and tired; there are buttercups in patches and sheets of glossy gold—and what matter if one cannot distinguish the points of the half-dozen varieties which are present? Really it is no pleasure to have the repute of a scholarly botanist without a particle of his or her knowledge. My learned friends quote to me Wordsworth's dictum—"A primrose by the river's brim, a yellow primrose was to him—and it was nothing more," but I dispute strongly the logic of their quotation. A person may love flowers without all the appurtenances of science. The mare's tail, waving in the breeze out yonder, has slender branches and no leaves of the ordinary sort; it is the most ubiquitous of May plants. I find it standing in water, along the marsh, springing up in the meadows, and even flourishing among the broken stones of the old sheep-fold.

A few early flowers have passed—snowdrop and crocus, dog's mercury, for instance—there is down of coltsfoot in the air, and the linnets collect it for their nests. On the edge of a sunk wall there is a tiny pale-blue forget-me-not, really a kind of scorpion grass without the fine eye of the correct plant. Anemone, wood-sorrel and primrose are rather difficult to find, though a few remain in the dark, moist places of the woods.

The quiet mill-pool is strewn, as with scent-driven snow, by water-weed blossoms; the water crowfoot with white petals and yellow heart is common there; and in the hedge there are deep blue spires of the common bugle, the rich purple spadex of the cuckoo-pint, and the flowers of the cinquefoil or potentilla. More striking but also almost displeasing is the great expanse at the foot of the islet which is covered with great rank rhubarb-like leaves of the butter-bur. The crowded pink flowers on sage green heads seem inconspicuous and rather dusty. And so I end my glance round.

To those who dwell in tents by choice, May means light and warmth without glare and heat, a softened air and fleecy clouds in the blue sky. It means more and ever more flowers—and a beauty which almost takes away one's breath.

Mud

Outside my tent-door is a rill, the water of which is needed for camp service. Its floor, however, is so soft, and the banks so crumbly,

"SPRINGTIME CONTRASTS": SNOW PEAKS BEYOND LEAFY WOODS AND PASTURES

that one has to dip with great skill to obtain a pannikin of clear water. Some previous party has set up a trough, using a couple of hollow field-drainpipes, and from the end of this we ultimately obtain the proper trickle. The little dam we found 20 yards further down the hill-side gave us nothing but interest.

We are not unaccustomed to water-side life. The pannikin has lifted up wee frogs, tadpoles (which are frogs in the swimming stage of life), newts and even wee fishes. The water-snails have been shaken off the reeds and grasses and sunk into the cup. Here we find little of life except maybe a green caterpillar which has been shaken from the overhanging bushes. Here is a thin bit of bark, probably broken from some rush; here a round dot which proves to be wood. And once when the cup was lifted quickly there was a faint curl of grey mud which had come over the lip and was being distributed through the water. The mud is too impalpable to settle down for hours; not so the sand, which comes from the next unfortunate turn of the wrist. One had slipped a hand-hold from the stones and the cup was used too quickly. The sand is just as hard and clean as the other stuff is soft, and it is a pleasure to come across it. But the little edges of soft rock on either side the brook give more and more mud. I believe the sharp, hard sand is from the rocks much higher up the streamlet.

Here and there a spit of clay is seen through the soft top-stuff; really the hill-side is covered with this material, and the brook has a hard job at carving out its own route. About a quarter of a mile lower down, it has, however, succeeded, and the result is a little waterfall. A ledge of hard stone juts out, the stream rattles over the edge, and a great scoop has been worn out of the hill-side beyond. It is possible to stand so far beneath the lip of rock that the water is a veil between one's eyes and the daylight. This sort of small precipice makes it impossible for fish life to come up and inhabit the mud. But the plants and sedges take welcome hold. One sees their brown and white rootlets stealing through the soft surface into a grip deeper below. There is no great security, however, for here and there a red sorrel or a campion, a foxglove or a rose-bay has tumbled over because the root failed to hold the heavier crown of the flower.

Now turn aside to mud which shows greater signs of life; in our watercourse the birds come only for a sip and are away, but out on the shelf of the hill they stay near the mud-floored pool, and f ed there. The place is alive with all sorts of frogs, newts, and water-snails. Every rush has its little colony of beetles, and there are whirligig swimmers beneath every big leaf. The water-mint comes up strong and rank, and from its purple castles of bloom fall many wee insects.

B

There are no fish here in the ordinary sense, but great carnivorous beetles flourish instead.

There are birds among the brambles—wrens and little linnets, with maybe a titmouse or two, and a scolding cry comes from the tuft which shelters the lesser whitethroat. They call this the fisherman's nightingale, but its voice is not unlike that of a fishwife disappointed of some pretty thing for her market basket. One morning a mallard was seen hereabouts, and there are signs of young water-hens. I wish that the little white-waistcoated dipper was visible on the hill-side streams, but it never cares for sterile waters, and is no lover of ponds covered with vegetation and floored with mud. The dipper prefers a white stormy stream, and pools which are floored with sharp sand among which the different cranefly larvae crawl. There's no stick encrusted with stones which the little bird cannot break in order to reach the insect within.

The mud alongside the pond shows many foot patterns, some of which are unfamiliar. Here is the hated rat, the brown, not the true water-vole; and once the sign of a field-mouse was printed delicately, with just a flourish of moisture from its waving tail, on the mud. And the plovers which we hear far above must come down, for no other bird has quite the same staggering imprint. In winter maybe a snipe or even a woodcock may rest here for a night, but in summer the place is far too noisy and tiny to suit them.

The hard crust of mud outside the pool is well marked with the hoof-prints of farm animals, but they are slow to venture near the water here, as the cake is soft, and more than once one has watched a heifer measuring the distance to the drink with its eyes while its forefeet seemed to be testing the swaying surface. The creatures can get away to the rill in the hill-side, and need not venture into peril.

Moths

> The desire of the moth for the star,
> Of the night for the morrow;
> The devotion to something afar
> From the sphere of our sorrow.
> SHELLEY.

As the evening darkens the tent-folk are troubled by moths around the candle lit for reading or for the last meal. The commonest victim of the flames seems to be the daddy-long-legs or crane-fly, which insists on suicide and will not be baulked. After various flutters, its wings sizzle, its long legs crackle in the blaze, and it falls quivering to the ground. I hate the sound, and therefore rarely use a naked light in my tent.

Quite a number of the soft night-moths may come to the tent candle. I have had specimens of the frosted orange or burdock moth; also of the ear, canary thorn, feather bridle, and lesser flowered rustic on occasion. But many moths are singed and fall, to be lost and forgotten. The ghost moths fly in the early evening, then drop into the grass as the air cools, to wait until the next night, when, before they rise, we hear the impatient whirring of their wings.

Beetles of many kinds swarm round our tents at night, but there are more whirling round the grey-white or bronze walls than ever venture within. They seem to be shy. The beetles which come out after sunset are either black or of some dusky tint, with weak wings. A tent invader I intensely dislike is the lousy watchman beetle, which will blunder anywhere on a warm night, and has a trick of falling on the supper-cloth with a thud as though stunned. If a lady happens to pick up the beastie and finds that little mites detach themselves from its legs, there is trouble! It adds to the indignation if one points out that the mites are really the beetle's sanitary gang, working off its joints the dirt among which it feeds and lives.

The dancing swarm of midges we see in the twilight are mainly plumed gnats, capable of giving some punishment. The true midges have hairy wings and bodies and beaded horns. I keep my lantern away from the watersides where stoneflies cluster late at night, creeping into one's mouth and eyes, and I hear the cricket and grasshopper holding revel in the meadows I avoid.

The light and comparative warmth of our tents seem to attract a veritable zoo of queer creatures. Between the fly-sheet and the tent I find earwigs, which do not show their wings by day but use them well at night. On the ground-sheet and tent floor there are ants, maybe in uncomfortable hosts, while woodlice and millipedes scurry for cover immediately a corner of ground-blanket is raised. Cockchafers occasionally buzz inside the tent sheets, and the bumble-bee rumbles so late and so early that I am not at all sure he (or it) does not stop the night as well.

Wasps wing home to their hollow in hedge or wall at nightfall, and the bees go to their hives. There is no trouble on their account.

And after dusk has thickened into night, we go out to find glow-worms, the female of which is wingless, crawls among marshy and wet grass, and emits a bright white glow to attract a mate, a plain, brown-coated little fellow who has the advantage of possessing wings.

Friends: Cattle and Sheep

Have you ever noticed the type of cattle and sheep passed in your wanderings? No, of course not; the camper is no agriculturist—and more to his loss, say I.

Campers, especially the light-weight folk, do not prefer cattle which maunder over guy-lines and bite lumps out of fly-sheets, besides giving exasperation at dawn by snuffling and trampling outside the tents. There is always danger that a stray bull may try to hold up the party—and then one has to be wary and spry. I never stop to argue with a bull; but then perhaps one recognizes the menacing snort and low at a distance and is able to get one's dearest possessions —not clothed in canvas, thank you—out of the danger zone at once.

Have you noticed the different types of cattle in a week of shifted tents? There is the so-called Blue Albion of the Derbyshire hills, a hardy creature with a coat which may be mottled blue or may not; then there is the handsome Shorthorn of the north. "Ye'll ha' seen many a less bonny face under a bonnet"—yes, that's true of the dairy cow of this type, a mild-eyed, peaceful creature with its only fault a desire to graze up the last yard round your tent. In Wales one meets the little black cattle, and they are consumed with either curiosity or fear. They either nibble your tent-pegs or depart to the farther fence of the field. In Scottish Galloway there is another beautiful little cow, and in Ireland you get the diminutive and shaggy Kerry and Dexter Kerry—poor man's cows, which feed on bogs where a Welsh goat would starve.

Most picturesque of all is the Highland Kyloe, a stark creature in brown or black plush which as a rule is good-natured enough to remain at a distance, but in a perverse hour can be most annoying. I have been kept awake all night by their snorting and breathing within ten yards of the tent, and at any moment expect that one of them would blunder up to know what one was shouting about. In other districts there are Jersey cattle, most beautiful deer-like creatures with equable tempers and a curiosity which is sometimes equal to grazing on an outstretched slice of bread and butter. And down the Welsh Border there are wonderful white-faced beasts called the Hereford, which seem to be all beef and big fellows (or ladies) at that. One of the finest sights seen through the tent-door is the rare event of a pair of big Sussex oxen at work with a hay or wheat wagon, dragging it slowly through the lane and across the fields. At sunset these ancient types stand out against the sky—a wonderful un-British sight, many say, forgetting that oxen were used for such work long before the horse was trained to productive labour. Still, it is within the possibility of the campers' vision should his tent be pitched in the right nook above the English Channel.

This is no attempt to describe all the different breeds of cattle—it is merely to ask campers and holiday-makers to take delight in such fine creatures—and to ask forgiveness for their occasional trespass on comfort. The cow-tribe seems to have no reverse gear; when accidentally one enters a tent and becomes entangled, there is no way out except on the opposite side, carrying tent, guys and gear along.

What about sheep? In the northern fells there's a hard-bitten little scamp called the Herdwick which seems to delight in lying out on exposed ridges and passes; it resents the presence of even a silent man on the path, but will come close to the camper. It is not, however, likely to be caught with a bait of bread and butter, nor is the black-faced Scottish or mountain-sheep. Welsh sheep are agile and fear the scent of man. The big black-leaded Suffolks, the long-wooled Shropshires and Leicesters, the muttons of the South Downs are too slow and amiable to be interesting to some of us, but they give the camper and field dweller some delightful pictures and rarely interfere with comfort.

Now as to horses, pigs and goats—one has a love for mountain-ponies and for heavy carthorses which are turned out into the camping-field after the day's work is over. The colts of these are skittish, wayward folk, and one has to be wary that they do not become unwilling guests.

Pigs and goats. Heaven defend us from such abominations! The first has the merit that it produces the breakfast rasher, but for the other there is no good word at all.

Buttermere in Storm

After a night of hurricane wind and crashing rain we came to Buttermere. All morning the squalls continued, gradually losing viciousness and persistency as the gale changed direction, and finally the afternoon sun burst through the scurrying clouds. The wind continued high, however, and we were glad to find a wood on Syke Farm where we could find a possible and passable lee.

With modern light-weight camping-gear it is possible to defy a fair amount of wind, but blustery weather sends sheets flapping, poles straining, and guy-lines jerking, and it is not pleasant for the camper to be threatened at every half-hour.

Therefore a rib of rock crowned with small oaks was welcome, and an hour from our arrival the tents were up and furnished, a meal cooked and under way to disappearance. After that there was time to enjoy the sunset, and to pick out the peaks across the lake. Think of it—as I write these lines I can see Red Pike, 2479 feet, rising above the doubled and trebled white lines of Sour Milk Ghyll; then High Stile, 2643 feet, and High Crag, 2443 feet, beyond Bleaberry Combe and Birkness Ghyll. Through Scarf Gap, where goes the path to Wasdale, is a vision of Kirkfell, 2681 feet, and the rocky nearer tors of Haystacks, which are about 1800 feet in height. Beyond a corner of these comes the snow-lined crest of Great Gable, 2949 feet. The horizon continues with the little nag of Green Gable and the long 2300-feet level of Brandreth; but in the hollow below this ridge the double white plume of a waterfall tumbling down the rocks into Warnscale Bottom is seen. Fleetwith Pike, 2126 feet, looms up next, ending with the sharp-fronted Honister Crag which overlooks the pass of that name. After this the view practically ends with the broad flank of Buttermere Moss, and a bit of Blake Rigg between which the road goes to Newlands and Keswick.

As these lines are drafted the sun gradually withdraws from the scene, and instead of rose and gold the distant fells begin to stand out in lilac with purple shadows in the hollows. The lake which has been blue is now a wind-ruffled green. This brings us back to the camp, for the First Lady, while on domestic duties, complains that three times tent-pegs have been jerked out. In such a situation the wisest thing to do would be to go round and double-peg every guy on the outfit. However, we hope for the best. As Flockmaster Jackson said when we queried this site: "It's third field beyond the post-office, and it may be all right with the wind as it is." If at dawn the wind-currents change direction, we shall be in a fairly exposed place, but this is not the time of year for gales blowing down Buttermere vale.

However, the night has now passed, and our tents are still in being; the weather has been fickle, and after dark we heard a few drifting patters which we put down to light rain. The gale never ceased to roar in the oak trees, and at early day we looked out—there was a slight griming of snow along field and fell-side which looked cheerless enough. The younger folk, however, soon found that the only way with such conditions was to run barefoot when messages had to be taken between tents, and work had to be done. In a few hours the snow disappeared from the nearer places, and there was a run to Cockermouth for supplies which the village post-office did not stock. I, however, remained with the tents, as the site is near the main road, and a mischievous person or dog can do much damage in very little time.

About a quarter to five the air changed; the sun was blotted out by high-flying cloud, and the air was soon charged with rattling hailstones. True April inconsistency of weather, you may say—it was not unexpected. The passing of the storm was an interesting spectacle, and the relics whitened the hill-side until sunset. Thus, and thus, we fare in our camp in wildest Cumbria. Between the gusts and squalls there are rambles out to Sour Milk Ghyll, to Crummock, to Newlands Hause, where the hailstorm caught the younger folk a-walking, and perhaps tomorrow to the hill-tops where we want to have a look at Ennerdale and the Pillar Rock across the vale. Perhaps it would have been wiser to remain indoors for another fortnight, and so await better weather, but somehow such a policy has no savour for me. Beside which I have to make my outdoor sojourns fit in with other conditions, and cannot pick and choose when or where I will go.

CHAPTER SIX

WORDSWORTHSHIRE RECLUSES

Braithwaite of Hawkshead—Sir John Woodford—Finsthwaite "Princess"—
Kitty Dawson.

THE most famous recluse of Wordsworthshire was the middle-aged gentleman who retired to Satterhow, between Hawkshead and Windermere Ferry, and was the first human character the poet Wordsworth tried to sketch. In introducing *The Yew Tree Seat*, he penned this note:

> The individual whose habits and character are here given was a gentle-man of the neighbourhood, a man of talent and learning, who had been educated at one of our universities, and returned to pass his time in seclusion on his own estate. He died a bachelor, in middle age.

According to the Hawkshead burial registers, this was "The Rev. William Braithwaite, of Satterhowe, Master of Arts, Vicar of Risely in Bedfordshire and Vicar of Burton Petwarden in Lincolnshire, Dyed at Hawkshead on the 8th day of Feby., 1800, and was buried in the Church on the 12th. Aged 46."

William Braithwaite owned and inhabited a hall of the Tudor period, which has now disappeared. He had gone forth to the world, in youth, dowered with genius, and proof in his purity of heart against jealousy and hate, but not against indifference. It was neglect from the world of culture (says Wordsworth's poem) that drove him to frequent the lonely loveliness, companion to the straggling sheep, the stonechat and the glancing sandpiper.

The younger genius learnt a fruitful lesson from this somewhat morbid companionship. The healthy boy's mind was able to see that, however disguised, pride is littleness :

> True dignity abides with him alone
> Who, in the silent hour of inward thought,
> Can still suspect, and still revere himself,
> In lowliness of heart.

Another "recluse" of a different type spent his "dull days" carving the rocks on the shore of Windermere. For years every smooth surface, every slab, was engraved with letters varying from six to twenty or twenty-four inches in height. On one larger red stone of at least ten feet square was engraved : 1833. MONEY. LIBERTY. WEALTH? PEACE. Another stone had the date 1688. Even larger characters told A SLAVE LANDING ON THE BRITISH STRAND, BECOMES FREE. The old quarry was marked by many inscriptions, such as, SUN. BULWER. DRYDEN. DAVY. BURNS. SCOTT. BURDETT. GARRICK. KEMBLE. GRAY. KEAN. MILTON. HENRY BROUGHAM. JAMES WATT. PROFESSOR WILSON. DR. JENNER ; also elsewhere THE LIBERTY OF THE PRESS and MAGNA CHARTA.

A later date was 1836. WILLIAM IV. PRESIDENT JACKSON. LOUIS PHILIPPE. BRITANNIA RULES THE WAVES, and in contrast, NATIONAL DEBT, £800,000,000. O SAVE MY COUNTRY, HEAVEN! GEORGE III AND WILLIAM PITT. One stone, at least eight feet square, bore but one word in letters a yard long, and that was significant enough—STEAM.

The legend at Windermere was that "John Longmire, Engraver" laboured for six years of his prime on this self-imposed task, alone, and in all weathers, and both by night and by day.

Sir John Woodford

Derwentwater had its recluse, Sir John George Woodford, at Waterend. He had stood by the side of Sir John Moore in his last moments at Corunna, and was on Wellington's personal staff at Waterloo. For forty years he lived at Waterend, receiving visitors on the lawn, placing hoardings so that the house should not be overlooked, and often taking his walks outside his estate by moonlight. Away from his stronghold, he was an agreeable talker, and a favourite with children.

Indoors he would have nothing disturbed in his rooms. After

dusting, books, maps, plans, models, coins, arms, etc., had to go back to the same place. He added a three-storey structure to the house, but it was left unfinished, without staircase, windows or doors. Sir John ordered that all rats and mice caught in his stables should be carried a mile away, and then released. Moles burrowed in his lawns and borders, jackdaws and rooks built nests in the chimneys, finally smoking out Sir John and his servants. Rather than disturb the birds, he rented a house in Keswick, and left the jackdaws to use Waterend. In March 1879 Sir John died at the age of 94, though he suffered from a wound in the instep of his foot, inflicted by the last musket-shot fired at Corunna 70 years before.

Sir John left the army in 1840, but was in constant communication with the War Office for years after. He was a persistent advocate of military reforms.

The Skiddaw Hermit was another sort of recluse. He appeared in Wordsworthshire about 1864, and his quarters was a sort of birds'-nest perched on a ledge of Skiddaw Dodd. He got home by climbing a wall, then dropped through a hole to his small room. He had a stone for a table, a bed of leaves, and wore neither coat, hat, nor shoes. He washed his shirt in the beck, and dried it on his back. Potatoes and meat he would eat raw on occasion, and he was fond of whisky.

This made George Smith of Banffshire rather a trouble to the local police.

"The Hermit" painted a few portraits, for which he refused pay. Further, he was supposed to have "religious mania". After his nest on Skiddaw Dodd was destroyed, George lived awhile in Keswick, and finally was taken to a Banffshire asylum.

Here is the story told by a Skiddaw shepherd :

"Whar the Skidda Hermit com fra we nivver knew, but yan summer we began to find ther was some body leeven in t'huts on t'fell as hed nowt to do wi' shipherds. But for many a day we nivver cam across him. We fand him at last in a ghyll penten' a picter of a waterfa'—an' a fine picter it was hooivver. But he woddent speak tull us. We thowt he was dumb and wanted him to tell our fortuns, but he was as sulky as could be. He went off aw at yance, leaving his penten and things just as they wor, and for a week or two we didn't seem him again. He was a tall chapp, nut varra dirty seein' how he leeved on t'fell, and allus was fairly put on. But though he gat as he wod talk tull sum on us, he wod nivver say nowt about his name or whar he com fra—you hed just to mention that and he was off like a deer and ye didn't see seet on him agaen for manny a day. He didn't stop on Skidda always, but he was oftenest there—it is aboot the whietest (quietest) spot in England on t' moor there. Then yan back-end he went off; he gev me a bit of blue slate pented wi' a grey sheep just afaoor, but I lost it on t'fell."

In Southern Lakeland there was or is legend that the Skiddaw Hermit painted many portraits for squires and their dames, but I have never seen or heard of one of these. The Hermit was often sent into the servants' hall at the mansions, and proved to be a copious feeder and drinker of beer, also none too clean in apparel or body. John Ruskin at Brantwood is supposed to have received the Hermit kindly, and to have given him money. These tales may have no basis in fact, but they are interesting to note.

The last Wordsworthshire recluse I knew built a hut among some tree-roots in the Stockghyll above Ambleside. He lined the room with moss, and might have become famous had not his madness become obvious. He believed that the country-side was leagued against him, and bought his bread from Troutbeck or Patterdale or Langdale by a circuitous route. He asserted that his enemies lay in ambush between him and the nearest baker's shop. Finally the recluse was certified as insane and removed to an asylum.

During the 1914–18 War Helvellyn had a recluse for a short time. The shepherds again found that certain huts had been occupied, and shortly the police captured a lurker, a conscientious objector who had come from some distant town and was declared to have lived for some weeks on the Scriptural pulse and water.

In these days a recluse has to be careful. If the police are not in search of him, the Medical Officer of Health makes pertinent inquiries as to sleeping-quarters and sanitation. The "liberty of the subject" is ignored, and the recluse may not roost where and how he wishes.

Finsthwaite "Princess"

Women recluses or hermits were always less acceptable than men. The most famous was the Finsthwaite "Princess", Clementine Johannes Sobiesky Douglass, of Waterside, near Newby Bridge, who died in May 1771. The "Princess" arrived at Finsthwaite with two servants in 1745, apparently just after Bonnie Prince Charlie passed through Kendal. Charlie used the name of Douglas as an incognito, but the lady never stated who she was, and ordered that no tombstone or epitaph should mark her last resting-place. She had wondrously fair hair, we are told.

The Princess may have been a mild fanatic who insisted on bearing this name, and she was boarded out in a place where she could give no trouble. There are other examples of well-born "cranks" treated thus in the north. According to Miss Wakefield, who investigated the story forty years ago, a Scotch thistle is said to have been planted on the Princess's grave after the burial, but the thistles are also said to have been planted by a recent vicar.

Kitty Dawson

In Graythwaite woods, a few miles north of Finsthwaite, lived Kitty Dawson, who used the cabin once occupied by her sweetheart. Jem Park was killed by lightning, and after that Kitty, still a young girl, took to the woods, despite her friends. When she was hungry she went to the nearest farm-house and was provided with food. Often messengers were sent with baskets of meat:

> When I went she wad just take the basket out of my hand, and empty it, and give it me back again; but she hardly ever spoke, and at most only said, "Good lad, good lad."

Kitty was found dead in her cabin by a shooting-party, and she was buried at their expense.

The two women who claimed to be "Countesses" of Derwentwater and Kendal respectively hardly count as recluses. While claiming the ancient estates of the Ratcliffes, the first "Countess" lived for a while in a cottage on Tyneside. After she was evicted from this, she took shelter in a tent erected over a road-side ditch. It pleased some people to believe that in this act she was taking rightful possession of her estates. The pretended "Countess" had many adherents in the neighbourhood of the Greenwich estates, in North Durham and Northumberland, where bits of excitement occurred from time to time on her account, until the Government sale of a large portion of the estate led to the collapse of the affair. The claim was too remote to be fought in the courts, I am told, and the lady's documents were not conclusive. I am not sure that she made a personal claim to the Lakeland part of the great estate, but may have done so.

The "Countess" of Kendal is said to have occupied a shelter or dungeon of the old castle, but I have never heard the grounds of her claim to freehold and estate. Probably she was a border-line case, and imagined her right to hold the ruin outside the Lakeland town. Charles II had a favourite whom he made Duchess of Kendal, but the title never carried any lands, royal or otherwise, in Westmorland.

This list of Wordsworthshire recluses may not be complete, nor the information fully accurate. It stands, however, so far as my research in books and legends can make it, true and full.

CHAPTER SEVEN

PAGES FROM LAKELAND YEAR

Green and White (*Borrowdale*)

My green is of the ice,
And my foam is of the snow.

GEORGE MILNER'S two lines pass through my mind as the
River Derwent rushed, curved, and burst among the rocks at my
feet. I knew that the upper springs of the stream were in ice gullies
and snow-drifts of Great End, yet other streams have sources as remote
and alpine, and never show pure green and vivid white.

The great gorge of Borrowdale has a wealth of colour in winter.
There are red-crowned oak trees which climb among the outcrops
of rock and have a background of dead brown leaves; the crags are
tufted with pine and holly, with ivy, yew and cevin; the water-side is
rich with purple buds and paper-white stems of the birches, with the
light sepia twigs and slender trunks of ash; with the deep, dark bloom
of alders.

The cliffs rise high—with bare brown rock here and there, but more
often splashed green and gold with moss either dry or wet, with red-
brown of bilberry, and dead red of bracken. There is parsley fern
too, but the upper fronds are browned with frost, and the dark root-
threads cling deeply among the stones.

Today the Borrowdale road is quiet. There is only a lad bringing
a small party of grey-faced sheep from Keswick. He himself is fair
of hair and skin, perchance showing the blood of Viking ancestors
like many dalesmen do. The flock travels quietly, for the sheep are
tired. As a motor creeps through the pass they flinch a little into
the road-side, but a mere wave of the lad's stick keeps them in order,
and the collie wanders, tongue out and heedless of work, at the lad's
heels. They make a picturesque group, grey sheep, fresh-faced lad,
and grey-and-white collie, quite in keeping with the great fells ranging
in front and around us, and with the white-fronted farms which peep
from cove and hollow.

I spoke to the lad about the green-and-white torrent hastening
among the crags: "Aye, I've been right where it rises, but I don't want
to see the place again. A few of us followed into Great End after the
hounds, and got lost high up among the rocks. It was latish in spring.

The snow had drifted between crag and scree, and there was a big spring running down a sheet of icicles. Every minute it would seem to ring on the icicles like fairy bells, and there would be a running down like tinkling down piano-keys. Stop silent, and the spring filled up the ice again. Another run, and a stop. I didn't like the spot, but maybe that was because we were a bit anxious about the way off. If we had slipped there was nin of them ropes and ice-axes to save us.

"Even there the water was green, and the ice was like silver. The water slipped into a hole under a snow-drift, and we lost it to sight, though we could hear it—or some other water—gurgling away down the white snow and black rocks in the mist below. It wasn't an easy job finding the way off Great End, for it was thick and cold, and the snow was that steep that we might have gone down the crags to Sprinkling Tarn in next to no time. But then snow and fox-hunting never did agree."

"Did you ever go as high as Derwent springs for a sheep?"

"Nut in winter, but I have been in Eskdale where they shepherd Bowfell right into autumn, and once we had to go back to the fell after about six sheep as had got missed in Green Hole or some other spot thereabout. It was wet, misty and raining, and we had a gay trounce, but the dogs found the sheep all right, and we brought them down."

The lad stood a minute gazing at the green-and-white torrent, then said: "T'sheep are nearly home; I don't want to run them with the dog," and so on he walked.

For a while I enjoyed the beauty of the Derwent in deepest Borrowdale, watched the flicker of winter sunshine on the white foam, the glint from the green current; watched too the passage of cloud shadows where the tints, though lower in tone, were equally lovely and desirable. Even after a winter storm the stream is pure green and vivid white, and glorious to behold.

Crossbill Stories

The first crossbills I met in the flesh lined the inside of a market basket at Kendal. The pitiful little wreck still showed variations of yellow, green and red about beaks and plumage. They had been destroyed by a double charge of small shot while raiding the last small apples in a Crosthwaite (Westmorland) orchard. The lady who had brought the victims to the town wondered whether they would be edible, but I could give no encouragement then—or now.

Since then I have seen crossbills on many occasions and in widely separated counties. The variety which resides in Scotland all the year, and is unknown elsewhere, has more massive, deeper and blunter bill, especially in the male, and the average wing measurement is wider than the migrant birds.

In Yorkshire this "un-English looking bird" is described as a somewhat irregular visitant and an occasional nester. They haunt fir plantations for the most part, and near the coast flocks up to 200 have been recorded. In migration they travel with parties of snow buntings, flying like them before the severities of an Arctic winter.

I quote from a forty-year-old notebook about the method of the crossbills in a fir wood :

Nimbly they go, parrot-wise, along the undersides of the boughs, climbing and holding with bill and feet. What a babble of self-satisfied, quiet chattering comes from the feeding flock! What wonderful means to an end in those crossed mandibles! Every third cone comes to the ground, but this fallen fruit is never followed by the birds.

Full of life and animation, their ever-changing movements are beautiful to watch. Their plumage is various; bright red, orange, green, and yellow, but not two quite alike.

Once, and once only, have they been observed on the confines of my garden; then they were feeding upon the scarlet fruit of the rowan or mountain ash. Their partiality to this food was amply testified by the way in which they completely denuded the trees.

The first written record of the crossbill in Britain dates back to 1593, when the marauders were described as

haveinge a bill with one beake wrythinge over the other, which would presently bore a greate hole in the apple and make way to the kernells they were of the bigness of a bullfinch, the henne right like the henne o the bullfinch in colour; the cock a very glorious bird, in a manner, all redd or yellowe on the breast, back and head. The oldest man never hearde o reade of any such-like bird.

The shape of the beak has made a little folk-lore of its own, summed up in the lines addressed to the crossbill :

> Your beak is twisted horribly,
>   'Tis pitiful to see—
> "I tried to pull the nails out
>   That pinned Him to the Tree."

The old record declared that the visitors must have come from som uninhabited land, "for that they at the first would abide shooting a them, either with pellet, bowe, or other engine, and not remove til they were stricken down. They were good meat", concludes th chronicler, but no person at a later date has tried to dress the birds fo the table.

At the time the young birds leave the nest, their mandibles resemble those of the rest of the finches, and show no sign of "crossing"
until they begin to roam the woods with the parent birds. There is
no doubt about the crossbill nesting and bringing up its young in the
north of England. They may not come every year, but sometimes
the flocks are large, and they remain a summer or two in our woods.
As the ancient chronicler said, the birds are tame, allowing a person to
approach within a few yards. There are records of some which allowed
them to be snared while feeding on the seeds of conifers, by means of a
horsehair noose fastened to the end of a fishing-rod.

In the Lake District, eggs have been taken. After large arrivals a
few pairs of crossbills doubtless nest and bring off their broods.
After a great immigration, the birds will remain in suitable woodlands
for two or three seasons, and then they completely disappear for a
time. With the extension of the conifer forests about Skiddaw,
Whinlatter, Ennerdale, Eskdale and the Duddon, more crossbills may
be expected, and some will undoubtedly nest and settle. They have
cheery call-notes, and lively actions, singing and preening their bright
dress in the most sociable fashion.

The nest is usually placed in the angle formed by a bough with the
main stem. The materials of which it is composed are grass, moss, and
fine pine boughs. The nest and eggs somewhat resemble those of our
greenfinch, though they are slightly smaller. The young, when a few
days old, are covered with a fine down of a dark greenish colour, with
parallel black bars.

The nesting season is irregular. Some lay in January or February,
others in March and early April (these are the main body of birds),
while others have eggs in June and July. The early nesters must often
escape observation, for in the first two months of the year, close
students of eggs and nests do not look for anything worth while in
their line.

In East Cumberland crossbills have been permanent residents
since 1927, with nests in a succession of seasons; nesting is also
suspected in East Westmorland, with birds occurring in many
Lakeland districts.

February Calm (Grasmere)

In February calm, Wordsworthshire is delightful. When the sun
shines the dales are warm; when shadows float over there is still a
pleasing mildness in the air. Even the nights are not stark, though
of course the high mosses and fell-sides are surface-frozen and do not
thaw till noon.

For five days the clouds have flown high, clearing the tops of the peaks, and between the masses, long, level, with a touch of purple below and sunny white above, there are streaks of azure sky, a dropping of sunshine silver before noon, touched with pale gold afterwards, and at sunset red with the lilac and grey of the fells.

The snow-patches on the rocky crests betoken the end of winter; the red tufts on the hazel bushes are promise of spring, though the dancing yellow catkins may be easier to see.

Each morning the reflections in the lakes have been wonderful. Rydalmere, from the rock known as Wordsworth's Seat, was perfect, every reed in the shallow being mirrored as to tufted head and hollow stem alike. The little islet (Green Isle) near the outlet stood inverted, its red firs and alders gleaming again from the water below. The rocky island opposite Nab Cottage, which was formerly the nesting-place of tall herons, was remarkable indeed. Though it is called Heron Island, it's many a year since I saw a jammy crane settling on its ancient trees. In my early wanderings such a happening was fairly common, and my head always turns in hope to seeing the blue-grey birds again. The island has a band of rock below the trees, and this, with them, is reflected. The little island beyond has less colour because it has fewer of the pines.

So you go by Whitemoss, looking across the reeds to Loughrigg, and tracing its lines in the calm water, towards Grasmere. Try to reach the Wishing Gate without peeping through the trellis of coppice oaks, and you will be startled, as I was. Silver Howe and the island are full of colour, and the way in which they are mirrored makes you gasp. The island has its few strongly tinted trees, its stone hut, and the grass pastures—every item of which is reproduced below. The mountain has firs and bracken, larch and oaks on the slope, scree and heather, blue hollows and purple rock, and today the reflections actually carry more colour than the eye-views. I don't understand why this happens—unless a thin blue mist just at eye-level rather extinguishes the colour in direct vision and allows the reflection to be more true.

Work back to Penny Rock on the motor-road—they are felling trees in Banerigg Woods—and the vision of Helm Crag will surprise you, though you have already had a higher view from the Wishing Gate. Helm Crag with its ruffled crest seems to come forward as we look across the still surface of the lake and to take into guardianship the village and grey church tower, at its feet. White wood-smoke from unseen cottages rises in thin strokes and drifts into a pall beneath the fells. Through Dunmail Raise there is quite blue sky, and the great shoulder of Seat Sandal rises to the right of its gap, red-

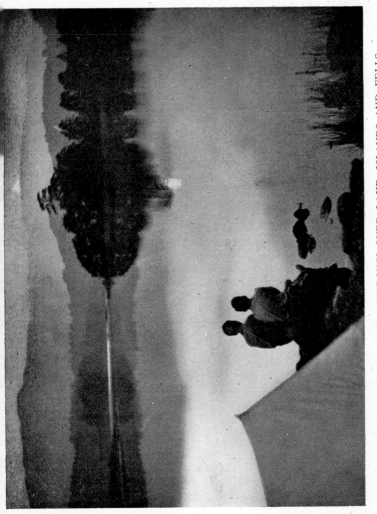

FROM A TENT DOOR: SUNDOWN OVER LAKE, ISLANDS AND FELLS

HEAD OF BUTTERMERE: EFFECTS ON A COLD AND STORMY DAY

brown at places with dead bracken, and white-grey of wiry bents above.

Wordsworth's early home at Town End should be visited, if only to view the peaceful fells in which the poet had so much delight. I doubt whether any of the present houses in the hamlet were in existence during the poet's residence, and his cottage had formerly been a lonely inn, the Dove and Olive Branch, on the carriers' road from Grasmere to Ambleside.

Sunset on a clear evening is always glorious. I watched the day of February calm die out from the shore of a great lake. The white-patched fells were swimming in rose and then purple as the light faded off. Again the reflections near and far were perfect; not a duck, not a bird of any sort disturbed the glassy surface along which the tints of sky and mountain, woodland and shingly shore were reflected.

Close beside me two axemen were at work, trimming a few poles, but mostly clearing the debris left by woodcutters and wagoners. Many of the broken branches had lain between lake and road for months, overgrown by brambles and twitch grass, and rotten. Still, the men started large fires with them, the smoke of which rose straight up to the height of the tree-tops, then floated flat, a blue-white pall about a hundred feet above our head. The contrasts of three jetting, roaring, yellow flames with the dark woods and still lake, with the quiet fields and the darkening sky, was great.

So I strolled home in the dusk. And two days afterwards the calm of February remained still unbroken. Yesterday the clouds, though lying in flat strata, with curly white flocks above, kept clear of the mountains. Today the light at eventide is stronger, turning the ploughed hillfields to a rich reddish brown, giving the lake a deep ultramarine blue, and lighting fires of red among the dead bracken. But on Helvellyn and its sister, Fairfield, there has been a dun white cloud which clings to grass and rock ridge, to snow patch and soaring peak. Four hours, and there is no marked movement. At dusk, however, a bank of purple crept into the gap of Dunmail Raise and made a long pack to the west, touching but not mingling with the afternoon cloud. I suggested that the dun cloud might mean snow and the end of February's calm, but the shepherd who had been clearing his ewes from a grassy plantation declared that it was "nowt o' t' sooart". It was merely another day of calm weather, and that "winter's putting on gaily weel".

Walking in the Rain

Either you must walk in the rain, or be content to waste many an afternoon. At this season the throstle is my favourite among birds;

F

the stormcock sings in the grey moisture and is not daunted. "Turn throstle and sing"—that's my advice. The walker can move on to- wards a hot bath and dry clothes, but the bird remains high among the sere sticks and lets the drops fall from its feathers. Bedraggled ?— not a bit of it, the bird is singing heartily. Things cannot be worse, on tree or road ; therefore they must become better.

The danger of chills is much preached but to the cautious and full- fed there is little risk. My friends are not lonely men ; we are all subject to gentle petticoat tyranny, but our demeanour towards the rainy day is one of unconcern.

One can whistle or sing as the long roads creep past. Always avoid crowded, miserable and glaring haunts, where moist clothing is apt to be noticed, and false premises are made. "Couldn't afford to take bus home ; it's a marvel that some folks can drink up the last penny without thinking of that." Well, well ; I'm a teetotaller, and on that particular trip we had not been under even a shed for six hours. No one pretends to prefer walking in the rain, but it's better sport than pining indoors, anyway.

We never halt while walking in the rain ; lunch or tea, or even a drink between, must be forbidden, and excursions into old churches and similar cold vaults are discouraged. Sometimes in the dark even- ing we keep step to some favourite refrain, but oftener, in the rain, we go at ease. Starlight or the moonshine needs to be enlivened by music. In the rain we are silent ; there is scarcely a whiff of tobacco, and yarn- spinning and those interminable ethical arguments about nothing are forgotten. But we are not miserable—until feet and limbs tire. And then one wishes for the comfort of home. Why all this harsh and heavy labour ? philosophizes somebody as we plug along.

What about dress ? Of course we are equipped with mackintosh devices, unspoilable hats, boots and puttees. This kit will turn even a storm of rain, but it does not encourage speed. Some youthful enthusiasts go to the extreme in thin woollens—the less there is to wet, the easier it is to get dried. Others are cautious to the opposite in heavy rubber. One sort risks pneumonia, the other heartstrain and rheumatism after overheating inside their movable turrets. Modera- tion is the saving spirit ; one has taken share in boots filled with water and even, after sudden storm, enjoyed a pool in the slack of one's pants. There are times when it is not advisable to sit down. Nowadays, however, it is easy to collect a kit which is light of weight, and so there is no need of perspiration on a quiet walk in the rain. Racing along the roads is a summer, not a winter, delight.

We who walk in the rain claim to be superior mortals for the greatest problem of modern life has been solved. There is never a dull day for us, though at times the best of field-paths must not be ventured. It is then that the main roads are again open for us, for the motorists are very few, and their splashes seem to drip to earth rather than scatter on face and neck as they do in merely damp weather.

There are rainy days when we go out to the hill passes and moorland tracks, across the downs and through the forest. These are really delightful in their unconcern. We hear the lark and the curlew, the plover and the waterproofed rook, but, above all, that splendid throstle which always sings in the rain.

Perfect Reflections (Ullswater)

A lady who saw the lower reach of Ullswater under perfect April conditions, with calm lake, perfect reflections of woods, fields and houses, with snow-grimed hills mirrored in the clear surface, strongly asserts that this is the most beautiful of the English lakes. Hitherto a stranger to the north, she had been taken to all the other lakes in succession. Windermere, Esthwaite, Coniston, Wastwater, Ennerdale, Loweswater, Crummock, Bassenthwaite, Derwentwater, Thirlmere, Grasmere, Rydal and Haweswater were shown her. And after the lower reach of Ullswater, she was taken alongside the lake to Patterdale, and over Kirkstone pass to the shores of Windermere.

Wastwater tossed by a mighty wind should have appealed to her sense of power and majesty; Ennerdale was a glittering plain of afternoon gold in front of blue fells; Loweswater, with its belt of conifers and the cone of Mellbreak, was homely; Crummock was stern; and Buttermere was wild. Derwentwater was seen through the skirts of a snowstorm but looked more impressive for that. At Thirlmere the snow was whirling through a gale which made steering rather hard; Grasmere had evening glow though headlights had been switched on at Dunmail Raise, and Rydal was a shield of dying silver.

Analyse these as seen under temporary fugitive condition, and perhaps there is clue for the lady's choice of the finest place in Lakeland. There was a sense of stability and repose in the views over Sharrow Bay, Howtown and Watermillock. The Helvellyn Dodds and ridges, the sharp Cofa Pike and the long wall of Fairfield were hidden in mist and gloom. The lady knows central and southern England, east and south Yorkshire, and the Borderland of Wales. She has decided that it is lower Ullswater, and nowhere else, for her ideal, but she will accept less than her ideal if the surroundings are those of Lakeland.

On her first visit she has seen all sorts, almost, of weather, except hot sunshine. The flowers have been denied her, and the glory of rushing torrents. To some people, the lady's experience could be rather deterrent: she has seen snow on the passes, has met cold wind and thin rain; she has seen the trees rocking and the lakes dashing their waves far up the rocks. And yet she claims that Lakeland is more desirable than drowsy Devon or lukewarm Cornwall. She is prepared to argue against the Cotswolds and Mendips she has been taught to regard as hills. And Dartymoor is outclassed by the stern might of Shap Fells when the storm-clouds hang low, and the gale drums against the crossing car.

Old Easter Yarns

In an old countryside we used to begin our Easters early: on the morning before Good Friday we searched out all the broken buckets and kettles, threaded them on a long rope, and proceeded to drag the load along the road. It was a noisy, clattering progress, and the lads hearing it assembled with clubs, with which they battered the cans, yelling a chorus of:

"Trot her'in'; trot horn; Good Friday to-morn."

The schoolteachers didn't like the rowdyism which crept into class-work that morning, and sure enough one or two of us would catch the cane. Our old master had a trick of gripping the short hair on the temple, which made the stoutest lad shrink. However, peace be to his ashes! He made a fair job out of some rather wild youngsters.

We always dragged the "battering cans" near to the school, and at dinner-time rushed out to take them on a tour of the hamlets. You could hear Easter coming a mile away! Usually the noise ended in some old mare bolting like fury from a plough or cart, and we had to run helter-skelter, for the ploughman or farmer didn't hesitate to chase us with the whip when he had pacified the steed.

Good Friday had its customs: the blacksmith would never touch his anvil that day, and in order to defeat farmers who would come down with plough-gear or horses to the smithy, he locked up the place and went off into the next parish on an annual visit. There was no custom against the joiner working if he chose, though the reason given, that Christ was crucified on iron nails, would have fitted as well to the joiner's timber in the Cross. Raisin wine and fig pasty were the customary dishes offered to all neighbours and visitors on Good Friday, and at dinner there was often a dish of herbs, generally the Easter ledge or periscaria, with nettles and sour-dock. One wonders whether anybody in the old country-side now keeps up this custom.

The fig pasty was, of course, an allusion to the barren fig tree which was destroyed because it promised the Saviour so much and produced so little. In the old years, when figs would really ripen on warm walls, it is possible that my lord and lady of the manor feasted on figs which in the preceding autumn had been in their own garden.

On our Good Friday we thought it wrong to indulge in any pace-egging or other Easter mummery, but the following day saw the play of King George and the Dragon out in full force. The cast was sometimes elaborate, but more often there was a bit of duplicating of parts. The minimum was five—old Tospot, who cleared the way for the champions; King George who fought the Prince of Paradise and brought him down in slaughter; old Jacky Brown, the best old doctor in his town, who brought the dead man to life again, and Mally Masket, a lad dressed in scarecrow woman's clothes, who had to weep over the slain "Black Morocco Dog", and generally carry the basket for eggs.

Tospot was expected to "stir up the fire and strike a light", and invite all and sundry "to see this noble act tonight", and he used a pretty big club for the job. The farm curs often jumped out at the sooty-faced, hump-backed fellow, and it was well to be prepared. I have known three attacks in one evening, after which Tospot went off home, and I was compelled to take his place. Naturally I didn't like that, but as I was the youngest I had to give in. No collie started on me, or I would have run.

After a duel with hoop-iron or wooden swords, the Black Prince would be realistically knocked out (one has seen some real bruises on ribs where the blow went true), and the old doctor was conjured to do his little medical stunt. In our north we held the contents of the bottle to be a mystery, but the Heysham lads declared that it contained "allicampane", and in a verse they proclaimed its wonders. Anyway, after a mistake or two (which all good doctors make), old Jacky succeeded in rousing his man, then

"Rise up, bold slash, and fight again."

However, this prospect is too much for the genial Tospot, who declares that the heroes must fight it out another day, and then he strikes up the chorus which appeals for eggs and strong beer. Well, we never got either strong or small beer in our Easter travel, but a dozen eggs apiece was not unusual reward for an evening of mummery round the farms.

I wonder whether the old play is kept in that ancient northern parish. There have been efforts to preserve it in its original dialect and to encourage its presentation on the stage. At Grasmere their pace-egging song and show was made part of the dialect play, *Cuckoo-Time*. Some time ago there was a representation on the stage in

Kendal, but the old amusements seem to fall away before the dull professional uniformity of pleasures in our villages today.

On Easter Sunday it was considered correct to wear something new, and to go to church. If you passed through its elms in old garb, the rooks would foul your head, we were told. There was, however, no such benison for one of us who had nothing new for Easter. There was a new tie between two; the elder wore it into church and should have sent it out to the other, but he did not, and the youngster crept along the churchyard expecting a punishment which did not fall. In these days it is considered altogether too primitive to consider our old yarns and proverbs : only the other day I got into trouble for telling some old tale to a highbrow lady, who simply deserted my presence without saying another word. Yet I heard it from her mother who told it to mine by the doorstep one fine morning in April, and there was nothing wrong.

Good Friday and Easter Monday used to be famous as taty-setting days, and some of my schoolfellows had their liberty curtailed, for the morning at any rate. But the rest of us made long rambles on those days. Easter is not too hot for walking along the dales and across the fells, and we ventured into districts usually closed to us by village feuds. Never heard of village feuds ?—you're lucky, for they used to be a terror to us. If a lad strayed from another place into our village, we had to harry him home ; and we met the same treatment unless we travelled in numbers sufficient to overawe opposition. Imagine the modern child stealing through an enemy village expecting a shower of sods or stones from some gang hidden behind a garden wall. There was some zest and savour in life then.

Our Easter strolls were therefore by lonely lanes, avoiding all hamlets, and then away over the moors and fells, among the grouse and curlews and plovers, eating our pocket-crusts somewhere by a beck-side, and then away again. The ring ouzel with its throat ring of white, and the wheatear, first came before my eyes on such rambles.

And then the view from the fell top. What, man, we could see the sea, and that was something to brag about. It was better than a cheap trip. But the fells were very lonely and the miles stretched far, and soon, despite all our brave talk and the encouragement of more food, we began to ache for home. It didn't take much to make a decision, and we streaked out for the little hamlet beneath the hills at a tremendous rate. If it took us four hours going away, it took less than two coming back, for we stopped not for brake, nor yet for hill.

Sometimes we brought back great treasures : once it was a bat we had found hanging in an old building in the woods. We emptied the satchel and placed it inside, carefully guarding against any escape as we stuffed in some fronds of staghorn-moss and of some ferns which were not known our side of the hills. I had forgotten all about our capture when we returned home, and Mother opened the bag. The bat had had enough of prison, and made away into a corner of the lighted room. She screamed, and there was some tumult. Country folks of the older type believed that the bite of a bat was poison, that the touch of its nails (or its wings) meant fever or ague. However, the terrible creature was glad to escape when the door opened, and off it went into the silent night. That time we must have come home late from the fell, but I don't remember the reason. It was on another occasion that we were caught in a mist, in a long driving shower, on the moor, and felt that we were altogether lost. However, I could not join in the tears of the youngest that time, for I was the one in charge of the party. The passing of the shower restored our confidence, and we wandered further away, to a point whence we could see a famous lake as well as the sea. That was the longest of our Easter family rambles; afterwards I took to rambling greater distances and, of course, went alone. The old village feuds seem to have died away, though now and again one had to look fierce or there might have been an attempt to "give this stranger a mumpin'."

In the years of milder amusements we went after daffodils on Easter Monday, and perhaps the older lads and lasses went off to the town where skipping was considered to be an Easter Monday revel between the rolling of pace-eggs on the greensward within the walls of an ancient castle. That was a joy which never attracted me, and perhaps the keenness on rambling rather pulled me away from company.

However, there was a joy in meeting the village fathers in the lane, and answering the question, "Where hasta been today, Willy?" Quite often I could name a point which was strange to them. "Aye, I've hard on't, but I was nivver there. What sort of a spot is it?" Often enough the name recalled relatives who lived at farms there or thereabouts, and I had to stand and listen to long dissertations about nothing in particular. Still, it was fun to gradually walk beyond the pale of the hamlet's certain knowledge, for there were many dales to which the road and rail services did not reach and to which one crossed miles of open moor or by bridle-path. That ramble became the greatest Easter custom of all to me, and I've never really regretted—except that I didn't scramble in a few more holidays on the roads and fells.

Colour of Mountain Tarns

I am informed that the colours of mountain tarns are largely dependent on the cloud-shadows and wandering shafts of sunshine and weaker light. To my mind this is a slipshod proposition. Most of our mountan tarns have their own particular colour which does not entirely vary under any conditions of light and weather. Looking down from the top of Coniston Old Man, the palette of Low Water is for ever dabbled with a green thumb-mark though Nature's artist may fill the rest with a range from purple to amethyst and even grey-blue. Further along the same ridge, almost in the next cove, is the dark-hued Levers Water, which to me always seems to have a touch of grimness. I do not think this is entirely due to a first impression of its stark blackness against white of snow and the streaked sepia of the rocks above. Goats Water has a blue tinge, probably because its rock basin faces south, but the colour can never be called warm. The great buttresses of Dow Crags with ledges of grass and violet-shadowed gullies are mirrored in the quiet if not calm waters.

Tarn Hows is glorious though it is not a typical mountain tarn. The plantations round its shores are mixed with trees rarely found in such surroundings. The blaze of flowering shrubs is also alien to Britain, and even after the blooms have passed the foliage is harsh, and not the tender green and gold of our Lake Country. Other tarns seem always to be touched with silver. Beacon tarn, near Torver, is a wedge or shield of more or less burnished beauty as seen from the height of Coniston Old Man.

The wilderness tarns are perhaps somewhat harsh in their colour, but they hold it better than do the lowland waters which reflect differing surroundings of woodland, pasture and arable land in every week of the year. Only Wastwater, Crummock, Buttermere and Ennerdale of our greater waters have the true and eternal touch of colour. There is little change except for winter snow and ice among the great rock buttresses and spires, and among the fans of scree. The water of our mountain tarns is nearly of the quality of agate, and able to take on a certain amount of extraneous light without, however, at any time losing its own individuality.

Dawn in our Village

Gran'fer believes that in his youth grey dawn found the workers in field and byre, even in May. Nowadays no one stirs to work until the sun is well up. When old Postie clattered his clogs at 2 a.m. to get our correspondence from the distant junction, our village must have held other Spartan folk.

I, too, have witnessed May dawn in our village, have seen the gloom of the woods turn to delicate etchings in grey, seen the cottage

roof turn to umber, the mansion ivy to green.   I was astir before the
first rook : had there been a nightingale in our thicket, its song would
have been mine.   Instead, the owls scarce ended their shrieking and
hooting before the cuckoos began to shout.

As I listened the words of Ruskin came to mind :

No air is sweet that is silent; it is only sweet when full of low currents
of undersounds—triplets of birds, and murmurs and chirps of insects, and
deep-toned words of men, and wayward trebles of childhood.

The bumble bee is astir, but men and children sleep on until full light
reigns in our village.

Somehow there is little desire to return indoors at dawn.   Nature
is distilling her sweetness ; man's ideal at this hour would be to eat and
drink and move.   Of all my garden reading there is one essay of Francis
Bacon which flashes a message among these generous flowers and
blossoms at dawn : it has often stayed my hand in culling a bouquet
which might not be prized.   He writes :

And because the breath of flowers is far sweeter in the air, where it
comes and goes like the warbling of music, than in the hand, therefore
nothing is more fit for that delight than to know what be the flowers that
do best perfume the air.

Our northern wallflower, distilling its riches with dew of dawn,
is, Bacon thinks, far behind the flowers of the southern vine, but this
dawn I find deep breaths of fragrance ebbing and flowing from garden
plot and orchard plot, the beauty of our village in May expressed in
bird-song, in flower-colour, and finally in a scented world of its own.

Crow-shooting

"Whar's t'auld gun ?   I'se gan'en to pay t'rent ?"

In old northern days May 12 was both rent-day and feast.   The
principal tenants of the old estate were expected to spend the day at
the hall, to pay their dues, and to take part in shooting the young
crows.   Afterwards they were regaled with crow-pie, strong ale and
radishes, with brown bread.

"Aye, if we missed shootin' t'young uns for one year, the crows
would go, and take t'luck wi' 'em."   Thus believed firmly estate and
village.   When a madam-heiress vetoed the May-day hospitality, the
estate fell into ruin.   Berryside crows flew over to Thanspot, and gave
the luckless Thwaiteses 40 years of prosperity.

Old country folk still have a certain awe of the rooks. Except for this annual day of destruction, they must not be disturbed. The crows know when the house is in sorrow. "Didn't the crows follow t'old squire to his grave? What, when we come out of the church, t'yard was black wi' 'em. And they went off, shu-ush, shu-ush with their wings and never a caw. Don't tell me they didn't know that he was last of the old stock."

Where young rooks are not thinned, there is a congestion and bickering as to nests and perching-places. The birds will fly miles night and morning in order to sit in the old place and the old company.

To pick off "branchers" with a rook-rifle requires pretty shooting. The overhead distance is rather puzzling. Farmers never decline sitting shots : with young rooks they are about equally sporting to the mark they present in their weak flight.

Rooks complete their nests on St. Valentine's day. In a month there are young birds, and these by mid-May are often able to accompany their parents into the fields. To bring down an "old un" is to forfeit 5s.—and this means spirits after the ale of eventide. The local pub does good business after the hall is quiet.

Crow-pie must be an acquired taste. The flesh is dark, and, except for the breast, very bitter. A crow-pie needs a good deal of flavour and masking. In these days a share is often refused. My last "crow-pie" supper was remarkable. Farmer cut the crust, everybody declined the meat, and there was nothing for it but liquor, cheese and biscuits. The pie was given away afterwards to an old chap who declared that he liked "summat wi' a bit o' taste like". Crow-pie is never short of taste whatever else may be lacking.

Night on Helvellyn

At midnight we left the main road and started up a rough lane with a beck gurgling in the green rift of the rocks. Not a speckle of white was visible now. The path opened, became grassy and rutted, and soon we were passing through knee-high bracken-beds. It was not a nice place to stray from the beaten track. The dusk, however, was merely partial, and as we rose higher it was easier to follow the route, and to pick out cairns and other landmarks.

In an hour the path curved into a definite pass between two rough, high-soaring fells. The clink of mountain-nails on the stones was companionable, for the brown and green of the hollow had disappeared, the light was grey and the ridges very close.

At the pass-head, we turned through a gateway in the fence, and found a fairly wide path going down to a dark mountain-tarn. It was too clear a night for legend, for the survivors of King Dunmail's army to come over Seat Sandal to drop his golden crown in the waters, thence to be dredged and lifted, once every year, until Dunmail is ready to rise from his chambered cairn on the Raise, and to reconquer Cumberland.

At the foot of the tarn we crossed the beck and walked up the grass slope. To our left was a path which zigzagged, but close to the edge of the rocks the going was more direct. Cool was the air, and the labour went easily. To our right the gable of broken mountain looked very menacing because it was backed by a mist of thin blue which overhung a deep and narrow valley.

At the top of the first pike we had a more open view; the mountain tarn disappeared, but we were in the company of great hills, and shield after shield of waters appeared in the dales. As we walked along the grass ridge, the outlook from horizon to horizon was clear, from the Solway to the north to Morecambe Bay in the south, from Cross Fell on the east to St. Bees Headland on the west. The lakes of Windermere, Esthwaite and Coniston, of Ullswater, of Derwentwater and Bassenthwaite, were visible and mountain tarns like Harrop, Blea, Watendlath and Easedale.

Right up to the end of July the mountain nights are often clear, and without the heavy banks of vapour which tell that summer is passing. The air is brisk and it is easy to keep the pace along the open paths. There is a sudden view of Striding Edge, a rocky bridge with three towers in its length which appears to be impassable from this height and in this light. Perhaps a party is walking along it at the present time, taking special care to keep to the route, lest they should have to scramble up a spike of rock or step across a chasm under rather sensational conditions.

Ullswater is visible below; then the yellow light on the northern horizon fades, and a dark bow rises in the east. This is the false dawn; to be followed before long by another light, which gradually turns from grey to rose and then to red as the sun comes over the horizon of hills. In a few minutes the daylight is pouring across the hill-tops, dipping lower and lower. We on Helvellyn top are almost first to catch the glow, but soon the air around is warm with gold, and lake after lake takes its flash of glory.

The Solway is visible to the north-west, and the hills of Scotland are beyond. I have seen the cathedral of Carlisle in a vagrant flash of light from this point.

The warmth soon envelops us, and we wait, enjoying the change from the sharp night air. Then we decide for the low country again—by Striding Edge, for the descent is just a little loose and exciting, and there is pleasure in handling warm and clear if not very big rocks. The descent to the neck between Striding Edge and Helvellyn is steep and loose but not troublesome. I have known it much worse—when snow and rain took a hand in making the way difficult and dangerous. The little notch between the two hollows proves to be a little rock tower which is easily crossed, and then there is a climb up the Striding Edge rocks themselves. The biggest ascent I have found is a crack of about 15 feet high, with a ledge half-way, but something happened years ago and now the pitch is scarcely noticeable. The path along the top of the Edge is well marked; if you like it not, there is easy travel on the Red tarn side. Don't get over the Grisedale side, for the scree is steep and loose, and if you lose height it needs a lot of labour to get back. The great front of Helvellyn looks rather bleak in the morning sun, but there are quite a few folds and rifts there. You will find them when fox-hunting, but they are not marked on any map or touched by any path or track.

Patterdale is a fine end to a night among the fells. I have known it for many a year, and have noted the slow but sure changes. The track to Helvellyn is now a trod, and Striding Edge has a hundred scramblers where, in my boyhood, there was an occasional one or two. I am afraid that some guide-book of the future will show it as the only route to Helvellyn; it is often said to be the only worth-while route up the mountain in these days. The best miles to Ullswater are down Grisedale, where there are woods, and Patterdale village always had more attraction to me than lead-mining Glenridding.

Wasdale Head in Hot Weather

Day after day the sun has blazed down on Wasdale Head. The little cove among high hills seems to focus the terrific heat; the well-used tourist paths across the screes and passes are dusty; the nails of one's boots clink on hidden stones among the heat-scorched grass of the slopes. Even the upper bogs of Mosedale are affected, and a mere trickle comes wearily over the rocks to the bathing-pool beneath Ritson Force.

On the Napes Ridges and similar rocks exposed to the full sunshine, the handholds are too warm for comfort. There is little content in wrestling with a steep, smooth slab when one's temperature is sensibly uplifted at every point of contact. The heat strikes through the roughest of tweeds and corduroys. To scramble along narrow aretes is to be laved in redoubled heat thrown off by the great rock-towers and buttresses. The upward look is less comfortable when it jerks beads of salt perspiration into one's eyes. For once the climber among Cumbrian crags finds that he may suffer from heat, from lassitude, and from headaches induced by the strong light of the heights.

The mountain-lover who is putting in a little rock practice at Wasdale Head before the season opens in the High Alps is driven to shady courses! That tiny hold which at Easter was just within reach seems to be very far away now; in this heat the best climbs are undesired. And the rocks seem to be dirtier than ever. Even on the cleanest and sheerest of slabs and pitches there is a trickle of dust which makes great streaks on the moist fists and face.

Obviously, where the June sun strikes hour after hour, the rocks become too warm for ease. Luckily at Wasdale Head there are alternatives. For the climber who desires shade there is the great cove of Hollowstones with the 600-feet crags of Scafell facing due north—a playground of ineffable merit, for the direct rays of morning and afternoon sun cannot bend into the recesses. There are moist caves on the climbs, and one or two springs of water serve the thirsty and eager man. Beware of Deep Ghyll—the little basin beneath the upper rocks is not constant in hot weather, and the easier climbs thereabout are very droughty. There is a cold spring among the screes of Lords Rake if you know where to look, but the stream which glides down Hollowstones is a delusion. The sunshine has deprived it of power to quench thirst, and its troughs have no relief for bare feet or lowered body.

The only comfortable way up Scafell in hot weather is by the easiest rock routes. On the Eskdale shoulder there are miles of scorched turf and a roasting atmosphere; up the screes of Mickledore is the torturer's way to pleasure. There are easy ways up Deep Ghyll on which the fans of Lords Rake are soon left. Truly in this hot weather the British climber discovers the virtue of "the shadow of a mighty rock within a weary land"—and he is slow to leave it for harder work. The descent of Broad Stand is easy in dry weather, but either Keswick Brothers or the North Climb do as well. Somehow one wishes for ease and straightness or escape into the recesses of the high rocks above Rakes Progress.

In the late evening, as at dawn, the sun peeps round the far edge of Scafell cliff, and shoots rays of genial light along the towers and spires of the front. One is tempted to stay later than ever in this beautiful light. The sunset gives new lines and colours to the soaring rocks; it plays puzzles among the coves and gullies. For an hour of witching twilight one can imagine that the old days have returned and that you are the first of all rock-climbers to examine, with wonder, a world of rocks hitherto unknown. But in these well-explored days, one does not get the key of a new ascent by some curve of sunset light along the cliffs above Wasdale Head.

There is a natural tendency to shirk return to the dale until the last golden beam has ceased to shoot up from the Irish Sea. Dinner-time at Wasdale Head, we mutter, is a convention for tourists. How we presume on old friendship and hostess's good nature to provide a meal at nearly eleven o'clock for one who is naturally aware that he could have reached the hotel at the ordinary dinner-hour had he so chosen. Perhaps there is mental idleness as well as the pleasure of the mountain heart behind this delay—for sometimes the little crowd at Wasdale Head in June is curious and even inquisitive on the joys and otherwise of the rocks. One is not always in the mood to respond to an implied invitation to "take the meeting, brother". There are experiences, especially at sunset, among the hills, which defy the use of ordinary words such as are vouchsafed to most of us. We may have the soul of artist and poet without the power of expression in colour or words.

We must go up to the rocks, hot weather as these maybe, for Wastwater is the starkest and least sylvan of our lakes. It gives no relief, nor is there anything joyous in the strong glare in the great shelf which goes steadily down to Seascale and the bathing-shore where, we are told, it is better to take cart towards deep water if you would swim and not paddle amiably about the shallows near the golf links. There are trout and char in Wastwater, but the lake is tepid, crystal clear, and sport, except at dusk and dawn, is at a discount. Rowing beneath the rugged old screes is at first interesting, but later becomes a task, and the lake is soon abandoned to silence and the stark, staring sunshine.

No, hot as the June weather may be, let us go back to the crags. In addition to the shelter on Scafell face, there are deep and gloomy gorges on the Ennerdale front of Great Gable, and the Pillar Rock, though it is three grievous hours away, provides climbs for every weather and season. There is even a storm route, disclosed and conquered step by step one wild November night, a terrific struggle, but somehow we have never discovered the place again! Perhaps it is hidden except in hours of winter darkness. There are cool caverns in the front of Great End, but somehow that mountain obtains little grace except for its winter climbing when snow and ice and spraying water fight the battle against any intruder. In high summer the holds are apt to be loose, and the ledges are often cumbered with scree and grit. Ridge-walking in hot weather is no joke—even a snoring breeze may be like a breath from a baker's oven, and the miles are long and hard.

No, it's the rocks every time if you would enjoy hot weather at Wasdale Head.

Summer Haze

Our British mirage—which is really heat haze among the fells—plays many an impish trick upon the hill walker. The most cruel of all is this : as you trudge wearily up the gritty, loose and oven-like Rossett Ghyll, which rises 1500 feet in a mile, a shadow appears among the rocks up the corrie of Bowfell. You are tempted to leave the harsh and difficult track in eager pursuit of a cooler and less stark locality. The shadow thickens as you turn a zigzag, until it looks like a black cleft of cave with refreshing shelter.

Don't be deluded. By the time you have struggled up five hundred feet of slippery grass and loose scree, the mirage will have departed. There may be a dusky patch among the crags of Ewer Gap to the right or a shade a bit higher up the front of Bowfell. You know that you have scrambled hard for nothing, for a mirage—and you are left involved in a traverse across hot rock-terraces at awkward angles back to the head of your pass.

To enjoy the fells in high summer, you must accept the mirage of drowsy but stewing sunshine. The heat is terrific ; there is no breeze ; and the glare is intense. It matters little for your comfort whether you halt often or push on, breathless and panting. The party which grimly passed you in the torrid zone of Rossett Ghyll is often caught up, either bathing in Angle tarn, or taking lunch and a long rest beside some path-side spring.

The shepherds advise you to travel early or late, and to take a light meal only before starting. They go out at dawn, with a bowl of oatmeal porridge and milk for sustenance, and they meet, in the lane, the parties who go to the fells after a heavy nine o'clock breakfast of ham and eggs. "You're too late," they laugh ; "the fells have gone into the haze a couple of hours since." Our reply is a would-be sturdy, "Oh, we know the fells are there ; we can find them."

But when you reach the fells the haze plays tricks. The conduct of the fells themselves is awful. They break all Nature's rules : Bowfell is constantly moving on our left, showing patches of shadow which come and go without bringing either breeze or mitigation of the heat. Pike o' Stickle peers over the foot-hills in Mickledore to see what manner of walkers we are ; it continues to peer at every turn of the steep path, a bleak pitiless face, the stare of which almost has the effect of a physical touch. How one hates it on a day of heat haze.

Until you know thoroughly the landmarks about a mountain-path, beware of this mirage. Consult your watch as to the possible rate of progress, adding one-third to the guide-book times on ascents only. On the other inclines you will have normal speeds ; you swing a bit faster downhill in the hope that by cleaving the air you will find a measure of coolness. The shepherds hold that, on hot days, the air does creep up the passes. This is not noticed while the slow air-current is just behind, but the refreshment of movement becomes possible when the ground is easy.

Check your position by map and watch—it is humiliating to go astray in thin haze, and find yourself in the whole dale at eventide. After all, the tragedy is not serious. Few parties go in for cast-iron tour programmes in these times, and "bed and breakfast" can be had almost in every dale.

In heat haze, the hills are constantly moving, advancing, retiring, resting and collapsing. Some of the progresses are dramatic in their suddenness and intensity. You pause aghast at a turn of the path— the gable of rocks and ledges in front is distorted and uplifted into a soaring Matterhorn ; again, through the mirage, casual marshes and tarns and pools gleam white and tempting as snow. You have to keep a steady mind and remember that this is Britain, and not the high country of Switzerland. Landmarks swimming in the haze are slow of recognition, and often enough you get a short distance (which has to be retraced) on a wrong path.

So the day of heat haze goes on until eventide, when the shadows can no longer be hidden among the rocks, and there is relief of cooler air. At such a time the heights are delightful, but many a party has not stayed up to enjoy the beauty of late day, and five o'clock tea at the farm has charmed them down the weary and rough tracks and paths.

The ridges, which have been soft and swooning, take sharpness and strength in the dusk, and long ere midnight the primrose nightglow is rising from the north and silhouetting blue and grey and lilac peaks and passes. Then comes refreshment and the tinkling of the becks among the rocks and under the culverts of the passes. The landmarks return to normal, and the hill-walker travels fast and easily in the glimmer which is never dark enough to be called night.

Bivouac among the Rocks

On the mountain-tops night is a brief season indeed. The summer twilight has scarce given way to the primrose north glimmer before the false dawn sends its grey across the land and sea. In clear weather

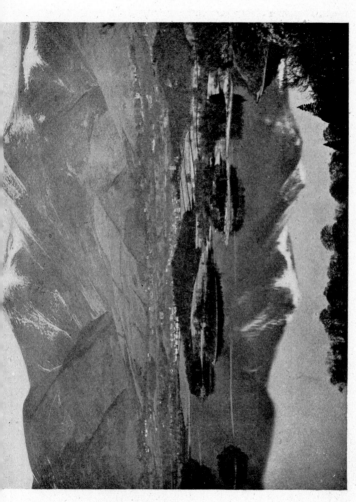

WINTER REFLECTIONS: DERWENTWATER, TOWN OF KESWICK AND SKIDDAW
MOUNTAIN

ridges, moors and open passes are easily tramped in the half-dusk, but there is deep shadow among the rocks, and most impressive is a bivouac there.

It is well to choose and test a sleeping-ledge before the gloom gathers closely; otherwise fate may send a hummocky piece of sloping turf where the bivouac is a nightmare struggle against slipping down and against sharp fragments beneath hips and shoulders. If scree must be your bivouac, a few moments spent in sifting out the bigger stones is worth while. Personal experience is rather against scree as a lodging, but sometimes it is inevitable. A hastily-chosen spot of green may turn out to be the mossy basin of a small but steady spring. The result is deplorable: you begin to feel the moisture in the coldest minutes before dawn, and it is fully day and more before you forget it.

Above one's head the great cliff shelters against the cold breeze. The rocks seem to throw off warmth for a while, and to make a cushion when the wind blows directly against them. On even the quietest night one can hear the air rustling and whispering among the high peaks. There is a tinkle from some spring among the ledges. How the cadence of falling drops changes: there is first a ring of distant chimes, then a snap of silence, a double gurgle, and more bells. Hour by hour the sound seems to sweep and to change its measures, broken maybe by the wind's uplift of the echoes of a torrent far below, of a waterfall, or merely a rumble of its own passage through some throat among the rocks.

Under such eerie conditions there may be little desire for oblivion. It is a joy merely to rest in the arms of the everlasting hills. The spirit is too alert, too exalted to accept sleep; the tired body may rest on soft, dewy grass, but the soul goes a-climbing. It rises above the purple rock-towers, up to the dim golden stars; these are mere lightships on the soul's voyage to the deep turquoise vault of the sky. On the grassy ridge there is always a play of misty terrestrial light; the world lies below like a sleeping giant.

In this spot beneath the rocks there is a different vision. We look up, up, up, and then—miracle of miracles—through the curtain of pale stars to beyond. The mind gains an impression that the world is in the making; that from this bivouac there is supreme vision towards the Might and Majesty which has shaped land and sea, mountain and stream, yes, and Man himself.

A wakeful bivouac among the rocks is not all loss. It gives much gain to mind and spirit, to the quiet understanding of the eternal verities of Life and Creation.

My own night bivouacs among the rocks have not always been either intentional or comfortable. Doubtless it is romantic to lie out in the clear open, with rocks soaring and bending over, but it is torture to wake up with snow melting on one's face and the world blotted out in a walpurgis of darkness and tempest. Dawn may show the rocks splashed with white, or even touched with blue ice-fingers where a passing rain-squall has been followed by frost.

Nutting in Wordsworthshire

From this hill-side path I look across an expanse of coppice woods, all tinted with autumn gold and brown, to Hawkshead, where the poet Wordsworth went to school. It is a delightful view, with the low-towered church on the hill above the cluster of smoking cottages, the blue hills dimly above, the lake in the hollow beyond.

At intervals during my day I have gone a-nutting in the haunts that he loved. You remember the lines in which he described a boyish holiday in autumn :

> Tricked out in proud disguise of cast-off tweeds,
> With a huge wallet o'er his shoulders slung,
> A-nutting, crook in hand,
> Was like many another day he thus employed—
> One of those heavenly days that cannot die.

Poets always do have fine weather and laden bags when they go nutting. I am not successful, but the beauty of this day will not be forgotten in a season to come.

As I ramble about I pick up a little knowledge about Wordsworth's hazels. The stems are straight and slender, and very pliable. The nuts do not all ripen at the same time ; one or two bushes are first. These usually stand out in the sun ; deeper in the woods the nuts are still of the green of the leaves with shaggy clusters hanging in picturesque fashion, and here and there causing the branches to droop by their weight. The size and even the shape of hazel-nuts vary, some being nearly round and others roughly resembling an almond. I am writing of the wild bushes of Wordsworthshire, and not of the culti-vated hazels, cobs and filberts.

Here and there a nut is really proper to pick—the husk or green outer-covering slips off at a touch, leaving the light-brown nut in the palm. It is a delicately shaded brown in hue.

> The sound of dropping nuts is heard,
> Though all the trees are still

was a poet's thought which came to my mind during my casual wayside lunch, when there was a slipping and rolling of nuts down the opposite bank of the well.

One of these nuts was double—and I thought of the village maxim, "Happy is he who lights upon a double Ash leaf, a double Hazel nut, a fourfold leaf of Clover—good fortune will attend his going out and coming in." I have found all these treasures, and in Wordsworth-shire too, but the good fortune (if a treasure of gold) is still withheld. I am called upon to smile at a childish memory—when we found such a double nut there was a scramble to claim "Cow and a calf, My biggest half", and the kernels were parted and shared.

There is a lure about ripe hazel-nuts which cannot be denied. They are hard but tasteful; if you eat one you want ten, and after ten, twenty, but they are never really nuts unless you gather them yourself.

I have tried today, but my luck has not been great, and more shells have been opened, and the white kernels eaten, than remain in my pocket to show at eventide.

Moonlight Stories

From the level road of dale or glen there is no sight more entrancing than the play of moonlight on snow-clad hills. The world above seems remote, cold, stern, yet alluring, and one feels an ambition to climb here or there during the midnight hours. Yet when one travels high after sunset there is little pleasure: at every step one is dazzled, deceived, by the silver rays.

It is then that one discovers a faint shimmering mist along the snow, just sufficient to mask essential landmarks and to make the map unreadable, a maze of half-visible lines without the aid of a match. Even among our Cumbrian fells it is easy to wander into difficult places because of the fairy beams. "Do not seek the easy places shown by moonlight," said one night-rambler. "They aren't there."

On Langdale Pikes we failed to "hit off" the steep grass descent to the gorge of the Dungeon, and scrambled precariously for a whole hour among screes, ice, and broken rocks. How the icicles tingled as they broke at our feet. Yet ever a few yards away there was a mirage of white snow, easy, clean, touched with delicate silver. It always vanished beyond a zone of deep holes and rock snags as we stepped in that direction.

To me a descent of steep rocks in moonlight is always unpleasant: the air is frosty, there are bits of ice among the ledges and holds. Even with a climber's rope such a trip is only moderately safe. "Light as day", "could read small print", are terms both easy and erroneous.

The shadows lurk everywhere; the cliff above, around, and below is distorted, and one can only trust a belay when its existence and shape have been verified by touch of the fingers.

On the few occasions when one has been benighted among the rocks it has been preferred to drop down some gully of deep shadows rather than risk a mistake on the open buttress where the moon shines so gaily. The gloom is already at its worst, and can be trusted. One party found it easier to rope down the long rock-face than to descend by orthodox climbing methods. The alpine line happened to be 150 feet, and the lightest man was dropped like a sack until he found a firm landing at 100 feet. The next was sent down to him, and then Number Three launched himself on the great rock wall. He had to find a place half-way down where it would be possible for the last man to reach on a doubled rope.

Safely held by the rope round a snag of rock, it was a weird descent. One's feet and fingers gripped wherever anything was possible, and then a fair ledge to the left was discovered, a well-known place with a good hitch for the rope. A few shouts brought down all the slack rope, and then the last man started on his descent, the line being held from below. Everything went "according to plan". Number Three paid out his line steadily, and in due time heard the scraping of boot-nails just overhead. Then he was joined by the last man, and the rope went gaily up and over the highest belay, to fall with a rattle down the rocks. A second effort on the doubled rope brought us down to the waiting couple below, and then we roped to the comparative safety of the screes.

In wildest Britain it is not usual to commence or finish a snow climb by light of moon, though now and again parties have been delayed, and had its light's dubious assistance. One has never shared in such an adventure, nor is there any desire to do so. The longest snow gully on Ben Nevis should be conquered in a few hours if in anything but evil condition and at all climbable with safety. A mishap, however, may delay the start, and the narrators become almost lyrical about the joys of mountain moonlight, seen as they scrambled out of the dark gorge, over the snow cornice, and on to the broad white dome of the mountain. One feels that relief has perhaps given a more radiant vision than would be vouchsafed to less mountain-tired creatures.

This is not a diatribe against mountain moonlight. If one can reach the broad snow-domes or sweeping ridges there may be a gloriously exhilarating walk, but shadows are abominations, and one seems to be unable to find the right crossing of any stream.

Salmon-leap

Above the dripping ledges of the salmon-leap, the leaves are slowly changing their tints. Sap and vigour have departed, and they give a sere hiss as the air parts them and passes. The grey arch of the bridge is patched with green and brown, with stains of lichens and mud; a yellow tuft of nipplewort here, a purple mass of toad-flax there. The cottage wall is white, but ivy climbs on the garden walls, and marks its contrast.

The first leaves to change colour are wych-elm on the rocks, and then elms alongside the roads, then ash and beech and poplar, syca-more, chestnut, and finally the oaks whose greenery in mass is still solid. The river-side willows will soon turn red and white and the pale gold coins will flutter and fall around the white-stemmed birches. In few places has Nature so infinite variety of trees to show.

Salmon are running up this short river, hastening from the last tidal pool of a winding estuary, choosing the heavier channel, and racing into smooth but swift reaches beneath overhanging trees. The river is quiet near the sea, but there is music at the outlet of reaches where the little trebles are sung over shingle bars, and a deeper, fuller note at the head where the current breaks over stones, and there is a twist as the current disappears and is lost for a moment in a sunken shaft or basin.

The salmon-leap is a mile ahead : the fish race up from salt water and rarely give a glance to fly or bait until they reach the roaring pool and its tail waters. Here the depth is so great that villagers consider it to be bottomless, that a body, man or sheep, drowned in it is never seen until it is thrown up, mangled and bloated, half a mile down-stream. "It is full of fish, but we never get any for a month after something has been in the water." I point out that salmon are clean-feeding fish, that their appetite in fresh water scarcely exists, but the cottager is not convinced.

The salmon-leap with its twisted roaring cream and blue current, floating froth and scum, repels and deafens, then fascinates.

So in a drift of water-dust from the pounding chute I stand and watch—aye, and think too. I remember those lines by Andrew Lang, best and most-loved angler-poet of his generation :

> A mist of memory broods and floats,
>   The Border waters flow,
> The air is full of ballad notes
>   Borne out of long ago.

There is legend and history in every mile of this surging water, and many a memory one would not like to forget.

Below us there is full tide in the estuary; from above the lake is discharging a heavy flood; conditions which invite many and heavy salmon to make a rush for the upper waters. Trout of unusual size are on the move as well. They appear as grey-brown flecks in the water, skittering and glancing on the bending current, and being driven back, with every fin a-twitch, to be rolled in the boiling water-pot again.

The sea-trout are silver fish, stronger and more inclined to break through the current and to jump over the top of the cataract. They seem to plough through the roaring water, and their progress ends in a little jump, after which they sink into the upper current and swim away. They are more easily seen from the old bridge above the rocks.

Autumn salmon run up to 20 lb. in weight, and their passage of the leap is worth seeing.

> Swift as an arrow glancing below
>   Speeds the silver trout of the sea,
> And even on thy autumnal flow
> The salmon laving his bosom of snow
>   Winds hill-ward.

Sometimes half an hour goes past without sight of a back fin; then the big monsters move, and three or four may be in sight at once, leaping out of the broken surface, falling flat on the bending current, and forcing their way with many a wriggle of powerful fins and tail to easier water beyond.

The sight of blue backs and silver bellies, of strong bodies hurling up the channel and slung back into the boiling pool is enough to tempt any man to become a salmon-snatcher, user of primitive spear made from a garden fork, a trap made of a woven basket, a net which is torn and savagely repaired.

I pass on to escape temptation—to meet a river watcher who was brought up as a poacher. "They're hard to resist," he smiled, reading my thoughts. And I agreed. "It's a big water, and the rocks are wet. If you were to get into a big fish in the current, the weight of water would jerk you off your balance. There would be no chance of swimming down there, and there would be an inquest a fortnight later when the floods had finished with you, and your body rose from the depths."

Green Mantle

Today I walked alongside a Lakeland river, and discovered an unknown gorge where the stream in half-spate roared through between shouldering rocks and finally escaped, all covered with foam, into a broad pool or wheel below. The song of winter waters is always hoarse and heavy, yet there are mutations, little runs, turns and sobs and scales, and to these I listened for a time. Then I came across a green patch, a cove weathered into the hill-side, a pocket of spring among the dead woods of December.

It was a surprising nook, and the green mantle so intrigued me that for half an hour I forgot all about the river's music. Anchored among the sodless soil of the water-side was a sycamore, bare of its own leaves but bearing a fine mantle of polished ivy which flickered in the weak sunshine.

The cover was not great enough to attract a wandering owl, though I have found them hidden—and jolly well hidden too—in a small patch indeed. The brown-and-white tree-creeper pays attention to ivied trunks as to all others, but it does not prefer them. Nor does the woodpecker give the trunk attention until the branches are half-rotted and can be delved into nesting-holes.

There are patches of green and thin moss, also of the evergreen or hard fern which one finds so often on low and level branches where moss and dead leaves give roothold. This fern usually fits its size to the rooting-place—short where the hold is poor, bolder where there is deep grip—but now and again there is a crash where the rotten branches give way. I have just seen signs of a foxglove star on a fallen branch which had rotted almost to a shell before it crashed.

The holly is typical: its low branches tipped with hard and sharp leaves while the upper ones are smooth almost as laurel. Down here there are no corals this winter: indeed, I find the woodland trees by no means certain in their output, though plants which are regularly cut seldom fail. The black-green yew is equally typical; in most places there is a distinctly fresh tint about the green mantle, especially near the ground. It is easy to find there young sprays which are both lighter in colour and are somewhat sticky. I cannot find that the winter moths give these sticky twigs any attention, nor that the night-flyers are more easily trapped in the vicinity.

Of the conifers I find the blue-green umbrage of the pine, a rose-stemmed tree which in England prefers the windy ridge and outer edge of the woodland to any place in the hollow. The pine is rather inclined to community singing: if you find one tree, there is sure to be a few more within close reach, and the notes of the wind among the needle leaves rises in a way which is undreamt of by the person who knows only the wind song among oaks or sycamores. Spruce trees I look for in vain: they prefer the warmer side of the bog where in summer they can absorb sunshine and get strength to grip the peat and clay in a mat of rootlets.

So to return to our green mantle of minor growth : there is a plaster of liverwort on the wet rocks, of moss among the soaking grass, and here and there stars and traces of other plants such as the common nettle, the dead nettle, the ground ivy (which isn't an ivy at all), and the chickweed, which seems to be on the edge of flowering.

Of course one expects to find green of watercress in the shaded spring, but is that, or is it not, the star of a primrose ?   Anyway, it's a small leaf with character enough to make one think of flowers in spring. I am afraid that the white snowdrop is not found wild on Lakeland water-sides, and that our first bloom from the bulbs will be the golden trumpet of the daffodil.

So the hour passes ; the foam rises and falls on the rushing river ; the song is repeated again and again, though one's attention may wander elsewhere.   And the last beam of evening sent across the long meadows touches the grass there to just a little green.   Green began the day, so does it close.

CHAPTER EIGHT

STORM PICTURES

Esk Hause

PERHAPS because I have passed that way so often and in all seasons, Esk Hause, the wildest pass in Cumberland, seems to be a haunt of storms.   I have crossed it in a living gale when only rushes between the gusts gave a chance of progress ; in snow-time when the white dust rose and smote direly ; in rain.   The last storm was particularly wild—nay, let me call it vicious—and yet so local that down in Great Langdale the haymakers did not cease work.   "There was a thun'er cloud behint Bo'fle and mist in Rossett Ghyll, and a few flashes and rolls but hardly a drop of rain."   Doubtless Borrowdale would tell a similar story, but on Esk Hause, 2500 feet above the sea, the stress was terrific : I have never encountered worse.

The day began in the usual sultry way ; little direct sunshine but air which became baking hot.   Even bathing in Sprinkling tarn brought little consolation, and the few who attacked the passes to Wasdale Head travelled slowly and with obvious distress.

Then a hot mist boiled over the rocks from Eskdale, and soon it was obvious that storm was breaking. There were distant growls and rumbles, then flashes of lightning, rapidly becoming more vivid. There were forked trees, and over Esk Pike, the play (probably glimmering from wet rock slabs) was a constant flicker. Then the air eddied, moved, and the mist gave way to a clinging rain, then to raindrops, faster, bigger, until the breaking of the storm.

With the wind now yelling, the thunder crashing, the lightning jazzing, the rain turned to hailstones, then to splinters of ice large enough to cause everyone to shelter behind the outcropping rocks, the cross at the top of the pass was soon crowded with hill-walkers, each in his or her way trying to shield face or head from the flaying storm. No one attempted to move, each huddled close and shrank from the terrific bombardment.

Shortly the ice flurry passed, the splinters ceased to whirl, the hail-stones were comparatively a mild enemy, but the mist and rain thick-ened, and the next rock could not be seen. The lightning failed to penetrate the gloom, though glare and flash were practically continuous and the roll of thunder rose to a crescendo, crash above crash, until the grassy ridge seemed to quiver. Then a pause, a gathering of silence, of power, and a final explosion which seemed to shake Great End to its foundations. The ground seemed to sway and lift in the final blast, and the breath was held lest some huge fragment should whirl through the murk and annihilate our little group.

"That's finished Great End, anyway," said one, with rain dripping from his face; "the great rocks have gone up and are settling down in a new place." The rapid, shivering whir which passed up the hill-side thrilled us to the marrow: it was as though some quarry were settling down, the edges of broken stones shattering and chattering in their new places; a sound to be heard but not enjoyed.

Is there more to add? The storm continued to roar and whistle, and to splash about the pass, but the mist never lifted for a moment. Thus we come, blinded with the flying drops, down to Angle tarn, cross the busy brook and passed over the head of Rossett Ghyll. For the first straight drop down the corridor between rocks for 400 feet the mist was so close that the rain-washed track had to be felt for with the feet, it could not be seen. And had it been visible through the mist it would have been difficult to choose a path in the ankle-deep torrent which was pouring down.

Then the air rapidly cleared; soon we were looking in surprise across the head of Great Langdale to the haymakers, to the great sickle lake of Windermere gleaming in the sunshine beyond. This was a land of peace and plenty—a grim contrast to the scene an hour ago at the top of wild Esk Hause.

Mist Kingdoms

Within the rolling mountain-mists there are kingdoms we are doomed never to reach. They always pass on—like the foot of the rainbow. Gaunt rock-portals frown beside their inlets, yet give us a thrilling glimpse of silver fountains, torrents of malachite and ivory, golden meadows, emerald pleasure-grounds, and a many-hued atmosphere.

In such garb one scarce recognizes bleak and barren upper Eskdale. The magic land, however, disappears when one steps over the edge and plunges down the scree slopes. The mirage vanishes. With poignant memory we recall in such circumstances Tennyson's "The Voyage of Maeldune" :

> We past
> Over that undersea isle, where the water is clearer than air:
> Down we look'd: what a garden! O bliss, what a Paradise there!
> Towers of a happier time, low down in a rainbow deep
> Silent palaces, quiet fields of eternal sleep!

Yet with the heroes, as with us, at the touch of man the paradise trembled away.

Every mountain rambler has seen these quiet kingdoms through the mist, and has felt that queer double desire to pry forward towards the reality, and to drop back with the vision unimpaired. Who has seen a ladder of glowing rocks rising from silver mist up to golden cloud, with a halo of rain beyond ? Don't believe (as the map does) that this is merely a shoulder of Great Napes sheering through the thinning sunset mist. Never will I exchange such a romance for reality. I have had patience with the disappearance of a misty "Plains of Heaven" which turned out to be the farmlands of Solway or Morecambe bay. Never yet, however, has the mist kingdom taken on for me the reality it had for Wordsworth :

> That which I saw was the revealed abode
> Of Spirits in beatitude.

When the sun-rays glint through broken clouds one can revel in many a mist kingdom. From Langdale Pikes the first vision to westward is often a delectable estate through the gap which leads direct to Cockley Beck and the Duddon :

Dim twilight-lawns, and stream-illumined caves,
And wind-enchanted shapes of wandering mist

in a perfect picture.

Once I walked through that mist route across the fells : it is an ordinary mountain brook, with more than a suggestion of crumbling iron ore in the bogs and among the soft screes. This I remember when the sun bursts on the flanks of old Snowdon, and shows me a mystic land. There is, ah! a delightful domain just away from the three crowns of Lliwedd, which nothing but dire mischance will ever cause me to visit. That great artist of mist and mountain, the immortal Turner, had a strong prejudice against picture-gazers : canvases were made to be looked at, not to be smelled. If the mists show a delectable Erewhon, be satisfied, and do not try to draw nearer. You will certainly lose by the venture.

Ridge-walking in mist is a thrilling pursuit. You never know where the veil will rend aside or what it will disclose :

A single step, that freed me from the skirts
Of the blind vapour, opened to my view
Glory beyond all glory ever seen
By waking sense or by the dreaming soul!

It may be Wasdale Head, that peaceful oasis of farms and hayfields in a sterile, stone land, or it may be the top of Gable, soaring so immeasurably high that one believes that its cotton grasses are flecks of high snow. What a Matterhorn our Gable would make if it were upthrust 10,000 feet or so! You remember that the peasant pioneers of the Alps frequently saw dim, misty kingdoms as they crept timorously through the high passes. The dim vista beyond the Matterhorn was a strange land indeed : drenched in strong sunlight, it had rich verdured forests and towers where the imps of Satan might dwell, and mighty caverns where dragons, terrific as those of Scheuzer, might dwell. It was really a vision of Italy, but the pioneers wondered whether it was the strange land of Heaven or of Hell's own depth.

Today, from afar off, I have watched the shaping and passing of mist kingdoms on the flanks of the Carnedds. The exercise has something of sadness for me. The fair lands feel no sorrow : they burst joyously from the white witch-fingers, then gleam in beauty of emerald grass and glistening bracken; they have joy in the bronze-green of heather, in the pine-glow of the mosses. Then, in a moment, the grey grip of another cloud reaches over the mountain wall, and spouting ghyll and curving pool is no more than a ghost in hiding. The next mist kingdom is revealed and departs, but it has hardly the same attributes, rarely appears in the same places.

What tricks our eyes play us! If, as the ancient philosopher says, man is born an animal with the ability to lie and deceive, he certainly has organs which trick him, when he so desires, of the truth. "Stand back", as the mist sweeps clear in front and shows a steep declivity, "another step, and we are over the cliff." There is a mist kingdom deep below—a shepherd land with tiny flocks moving about the grass patches and by the gushing streams. If you recognize the place before the eye speeds terror to the brain, you can smile at a danger which really doesn't exist. Otherwise you get an impression not easily shaken off.

My first acquaintance with the great rocks and tiny tarns of Cwm Glas was from the heights of Crib Goch on a day of mist, snow and rain. How immeasurably deep and pleasant seemed those still dark shields of water from this cold and moist footing on a narrow rock-ridge. The distance seemed miraculous, even for the magic land of Wales. Less than 3000 feet it could not be, from this Arctic cold to that dancing sunshine patch in the foot of the pass. Indeed, a pilgrimage to Snowdon was specially made by that fine rock-girt route which skirts the Parson's Nose and other cliffs before I could entirely free my mind from the chains of that enthralling mist vision.

Our ears conspire to trick us in the mist. Who has not heard the rattle of kettledrums, the wailing of fifes, the strange hush-hush of marching feet as the mist crawled and writhed among the rock-towers? There was a swifter current of air, and the music turned to a lilt of fairy bagpipes. The mists burst aside as though to show the pageant of some distant kingdom, but before the last veil had parted we were again in the whirling grey-white cloud. "Just beyond" is ever the tragedy of human life; we cannot grip the iridescence of a shifting cloud, the peace of a mist kingdom. Our dull ears often sense rather than hear the concourse of sounds.

Mist kingdoms are not always downwards, nor yet across the great gullies. Sometimes they are in the height, majestic and mysterious. We have seen visions in the clouds, of earth uplifted to form magic realms. A distant county seems to rise higher and higher, then to disappear in the azure blue of the northern sky. Shadowy monsters seem to trail across our mist kingdoms; masses which are fluid and not material, horses and chariots and battalions impressive upon one's consciousness yet without the power of touch.

My mist kingdoms are always at peace. There is a pageantry of

joy that gloom and war of the lower elements have passed away
Though they are but realms of a moment, their spirit is not dashed by
premonition of tragedy, of futility. For the moment they are realms
of delight, of beauty, of myriad colours, of settled peace and order.
Indeed, the whole mountain-land speaks of calm settlement, though
wind and rain buffet, thunders roll, and the lightning flashes and
shatters. Tomorrow the hill-side may have one more tiny scar, a rent
where the rock-ledge has slipped, a mud-trail, a fan of fresh pebbles
where a flooded stream has washed a new course through the glacial
drift. But the mountains still hold the same eternal and holy peace,
still on their flanks and in their mighty bosoms the wandering clouds
and the storm-lights will build up those mist kingdoms which are ever
for the eye, the ear and the brain, but never for the foot or the hand.

Music of the Hills

Every mountain, I contend, has its own storm music. We who have
been privileged to wander on many peaks in wild weather rejoice in
our memories of varying storm song. There is Skiddaw, a meek old
giant with the wind mumbling over his rounded shoulders, and never
the squeak of a fife in his mumbling orchestra. Blencathra, or Saddleback, recalls, on a day of south-easterly storm, the galloping horses of
Border raids; their hooves thunder in its coves and on the sharp stony
edges there is the thin scream of cavalry trumpets.

This is John Peel's country, and I would far rather hear the chanting
of spectral hounds and huntsmen, but really that music is more typical
of the Eskdale fells where the winds twist among the ridges of Scafell,
Scafell Pike, Bowfell and Great End. More than once have I halted on
the wilderness tracks on a wild evening, and wondered whether hounds
were afoot, hunting in untimely hours and weather. Even a fells fox-
hound cannot follow a scent through a living gale and a tippling rain-
storm.

On Esk Hause I met a party of shepherds : they had lost the hunt in
the thick cloud, and were arguing about their bearings. Then one
said : "That's Bowfell sounding, anyway ; I could tell it on the darkest
night in winter." My ears are not so closely attuned to the heights,
but the compass checked off that Bowfell lay exactly in the direction
pointed with his finger.

It is not my intention to catalogue our Cumbrian peaks and their
music, though it would be delightful to do it. Great Gable strikes a
high note as the gale shrieks over the ridges of its sharp pyramid.
Scafell has thunder in its riven gullies—they seem to echo the wind, for

only when the storm comes from the north do they get any direct blasts. Scafell Pike sings of piled rock and scree and grass. And what of Helvellyn—there you get a whole mountain orchestra. No other peak seems to hold the same hollow notes as the storm twists into Keppel Cove or Red tarn or up Grisedale to meet the "dark brow" of the great mass. On many a windy day the crossing of Striding Edge is perilous : indeed, even in a strong breeze the exposed towers of rock are usually avoided and the path round their bases is followed. But the rock-towers are part of the great organ orchestra : they produce the sharp high note in the stream of humming sound, as the air is driven over and against the giant cliffs.

When the storm comes from the west, the coves and rock-towers are comparatively silent, but the music along the grassy tops and up the folded hill-side is like the rustling of mighty reeds. The storm is broken by its passage over Armboth fells, and the gulf in which Thirlmere lies 2500 feet below hardly balances the rugged gusts. I admit that Helvellyn in storm has a fascination for me : it was up there that my first night-gale on the fells was met, and the drumming of its squalls against my ears, then a new sensation, will not be forgotten. I have ventured on Helvellyn in winter when gale, ice and snow made its conquest a delicious torment. There are days when the easy track from Wythburn church is almost forbidden to the wanderer who has not tramped his ten miles through pouring rain to reach the mountain. I boast that in my young days a march of twenty miles to Wythburn made the ascent of the peak much more desired than it can be to a generation who use everything but their feet as a means of progress to the stormy hills.

Wastwater in Gale

At Wasdale Head I always revel in the gale, and keep a sharp lookout for Nature under stress of storm. The little knot of houses at the last level of the stretch is really sheltered ; the comb of Yewbarrow turns off the hurricane squalls which race and roar up the lake, and a shoulder of Lingmell sweeps across the gales from Styehead pass. In mid-April the snow is usually confined to a few drifts on the highest fells, and to such rock fissures as Deep Ghyll in Scafell or the north-facing gullies of Great End.

Such snow needs finding and reaching too ; but the gale is always ready for a wrestle if you step outside the threshold, and it will continue the game for hours.

Sometimes it dodges away and shouts outside the larch plantations, but it always lies in wait and jerks out on you at some unexpected place.

I love an April gale, and always desire to go into it bareheaded, bare-throated, and with a jolly welcome for its hard blows.

Last evening Wastwater was scourging itself to wrath. The little rock bays about Bowderdale beck were casting up constant jets of white, but this morning the lake sweeps in long waves, a score yards from crest to crest, and every reef spouts in turn. The long strand at the head of the lake is a bar of seething foam, and there is a foot-high mass of wreckage, leaves, grass, and broken sticks.

It is still winter at Wasdale Head. The little gorge by Ritson Force has very few primroses and celandines; even daisies are scarce. The aspect of those fields between the thick stone walls is storm-beaten; the yews round the little church are all the green except maybe a little smoke among the larches. The bracken still stands in russet wet beds on the hill-sides, and the parsley fern, though the little balls of green thread—next year's fronds—may be in hiding, are dry and dead of upper fronds. The willows and ashes and alders which root among the water-borne boulders in the level valley are bare of leaf, even of promising buds.

The only colour along the ground is that of gorse; the flank of Yewbarrow which extends down to the lake-side seems to have some element favouring this growth, for acres of blossom are visible, chiefly near the road, during the entire year. I have never approached Was-dale without knowing the truth of the old maxim: "When the gorse is out of bloom, kissing is out of fashion."

This wild morning the nearest hills are touched with a lilac mottle which the dales-folk always recognize as sign of high wind. There is roar of many waters in the dale, where every brook is bank-high and more, but still greater is the roar from above where the gale is striking against the mighty peaks and ridges. You can hear the strong boom as each blast strikes into some deep cove, the sharper note when it breaks against a mighty cliff. Yes, and when we go aloft into the storm there will be screaming and whistling and shouting, pushing and pulling and lifting, to your heart's content.

The last touch of green fern is left with the farmland; after this, April is merely a tinge of moss and lichen, of some wonderful patterns and communities, of moss like tiny firs or spruces, like filmy ferns; of lichens in all colours, red, crimson, yellow and green as well as the grey silver which we expect. I have a fancy for lichens, but do not under-stand either their structure or their varieties. Some, I am told, are mere vegetables, growing in a lifetime to the extent of 100 per cent of area, while others are retiring, aristocratic, and have a way of growing a mere film in every generation of mankind. It's queer, looking at these lichens on the rock wilderness of Mickledore. They have not the thickness of sea-rock lichen, which can be felt on the edge of the stone ; they grow slowly but surely ; they seem to be almost more stable in form than the hills around them, for weather is always breaking down slabs and crests, shattering the boulders into scree, the scree into mud which goes into Wasdale below to make the fields.

In this wild weather, few birds are to be found among the mountain-tops. Only the raven and carrion crow keep the heights in winter, and they have to glance to the low country for their carrion meals. There is nothing to eat on Esk Hause in winter, and the sharp wind sweeps even these birds away in its grip. The only bird which in my mind is master of an Easter gale is the buzzard. In size this is equal to many a small eagle, and its wing-power is tremendous. I watched the bird rise from the depths near Sprinkling tarn, curve alongside the cliffs of Great End, and then sweep out of shelter. The gale at ground level was enough to knock us off our feet, but the buzzard met it easily ; there was merely a turn of those brown-tipped ashen wings, a sort of curving glide, and the bird went out of sight over Esk Pike, and away to some corrie of Bowfell.

There are days when the raven keeps close to the rocks, and the carrion crow uses its perch on a blasted oak above the farms, when every bird is almost out of sight. The gulls, seen on the high passes, are merely seabird travellers from one coast to the other, and they have to be able to drive through blasts sufficient to shatter the wings of a land bird. They contrive to pass through the wicked gusts by a cunning and skilful method of using the curve of one wind-stream to carry them forward and across another. I have watched several pairs of gulls on Styhead pass, and they get away into the wind where the land birds would be content to travel cross-way or to wait awhile.

And there is no wilder sound in bird-life than the laughing scream of the gull which has battled over the pass, and can see the shelving sea far beyond. "Hech-hech-hech" it goes with a weird mocking intensity.

The small birds have not returned to their summer haunts : I look in vain for wheatears, mountain pipits, larks, and the like. Some are still in the warm south, others in the glens and dales. They can afford to wait until the April hurricanes rage out their worst, and until the warm sunshine comes to the Lake Country once more.

I love high wind ; the struggle with the elements on such a day as this is more interesting than the search for mythical snow-drifts, hidden in the mists, or for rock- and ice-climbs among the deep gullies of the fells where there is far more water than is necessary for comfort. And at the end the wind has its last blow as we turn into the open court in front of our hotel, and staggers us as we reach its very threshold.

GATHERING BRACKEN AT THIRLMERE: HELVELLYN IN BACKGROUND

"SALMON LEAP", FORCE FALLS, NEAR KENDAL.

When the Rope Goes Tight

Rock-climbers are not fond of writing about their failures. In reading of great conquests, one feels sure that the narrator's enthusiasm selects the movements which solved the difficult problem and brought about triumph. The great effort is depicted in highlights; the failures are faintly seen through a few shadowy words, or ignored altogether. Often enough it is only when the keen reader adds together the total time taken on the ascent that he discovers that at least a couple of hours of unsuccessful effort have been forgotten.

You must enter the inner circle of climbers before much information about "discrepancies" is disclosed. I recall a vivid hint about a Pillar Climb undertaken on a damp and dismal day. The leader threaded the rope through a hole in some rocks, and tried to balance delicately to a fair hold several feet away. He was too chilled. "I'm coming off," he called casually, and in a flash the rope went tight. He had slipped several feet down the holdless rock-wall, and the rope swung him in like a pendulum. At a further attempt the pitch was conquered.

The sensation of falling from the rocks is horrible; that of being stopped by a rope is sometimes worse. Of course one does not topple outwards or headlong, whatever the stories may say. If a man dropped a dozen feet sheer either the rope would break or his spine would snap at the jerk. "Coming on to the rope" means usually a nasty scrape on one's ribs, and one has carried the mark for months afterwards.

To watch a man miss his hold or slip from a ledge is too busy a job to be funny. The rope must come in at once, or the other will suffer a nasty jerk. The belay must be sound, else one's hands are pulled forward, and there is a gory mess as knuckles are ground against hard stone. No climber allows the rope to run out until there is pressure on the loop round his waist. In most cases he would be jerked off like a sack of potatoes.

I want to mention one experience—its only merit is that it happened long ago. It was a scratch party; one fair climber, a good but injudicious climber, two ladies, and finally the writer, who was an unknown quantity. The course was a simple rock traverse. The fair man went along with the leader in front of the ladies. He insisted that they should not move until he gave the word. He called round the corner for the first one to take a rather delicate bit, when the second made a mis-step, slipped and came on the rope. Of course the lady in front was peeled from the rock, and both slipped down the sloping face. My yell caused the leader to haul in hard and fast, and for some

H

seconds we seemed to hang on the line, grimly doing our utmost to keep control. At every moment I feared the rope would slip off my belay, in which case doubtless I would have joined the ladies somewhere below. It was a nasty moment or two. Then the first lady gripped most pluckily on some rough rock, but the criminal seemed helpless and hopeless. She had resigned herself to eternal smash, and would take no further interest.

Luckily I was in a position to double-fasten my belayed rope, and we were "checkmate", whatever that is. The ladies were on the line, but we could not pull them up. The position was no longer critical—for us. Then the damsel below began to take interest in life, and to grip a rock ledge, thus taking her weight off my line. I would then consider some method of hauling her in, and did so, inch by inch, assisting her rather too roughly to regain the ledge from which she had slipped.

We completed the climb, but the lady never forgave me for the strenuous jerks on the line which roused her to effort. I think that the sum total of her contusions were hidden—mine were very evident and gory indeed.

The climber is lucky who has no experience of the rope going tight round his body, or round the belay in front or behind. In every long expedition there is some likelihood that the leader or other climber may not get quite home, and have to be assisted in this manner to make a new and successful effort.

Winter Colour

To the mountains rather than to the valleys is granted the pageant of winter colour. Snow masks the last shred of beauty from pasture and meadow, chills the glow from woodland, lake and river, but it reveals the glory of high places. Let me quote the words of Robert Southey, who was not then a willing admirer of the beauty of the Keswick district in which he had just settled :

The very snow, which you would perhaps think would monotonize the mountains, gives new varieties; it brings out their recesses and designates all their inequalities . . . and it reflects such tints of saffron, or fawn, or rose colour to the evening sun.

There is colour at dawn and noon, aye, and at midnight too, when the great peaks stand out like modelled ivory against the dark-blue horizon, or are spectral white in the dim moonlight. You must see winter colour to understand, and on a clear December day, with snow on the heights, there is ample opportunity for the study.

Get away from the dale as early as possible. A sunrise from Styhead pass is worth a dozen mornings in Borrowdale or Wasdale or Langdale. The sky to the east may be grey and the distant white peaks half visible through the gloom. Then comes the sun, at first a mere shimmer of light, then a distorted pale orb shining with an appearance of meekness, but remembering that "the meek shall inherit the earth", he grows bold, and golden bars wave up the sky, touching the few flecks of high cloud. Already the snowy hills are taking up the glory, and belts of rose, gold and yellow seem to pass in and out of the great shadowy hollows. Indeed, I have to keep my foot down hard on reality, else I should swear that the running, rising, flowing lights had their source this side of the white ranges and were quite separate from the feeble sun which is rising on the other side of the Pennine moors.

Does the pageant fade when the sun is in full vision ? No : in winter the country-side, and especially the high fells, is not like Coleridge's summer accusation—"a theatre at noon", with every passion and artifice discovered in the staring light, and no mystery, no secret anywhere. Is there not a faint blue mist in Mickledore, through which the rock ribs of Scafell are thrusting to their white crowns ; is there not a plume of white tinted with rose waving about the head of Helvellyn and looking as though at any moment it may break loose and float away.

As we crunch up the frozen buttress of Great Gable, Wastwater seems to be garish below, then of a sudden it is hidden in a mist of glittering particles ; it is lost, it is found again and again, a dark shield against the crumpled white screes. The mist-cloud creeps round the sharp pyramid of Great Gable for a few minutes ; it is piercing cold, white and confusing. Every landmark is hidden or changed in its embraces. Yet there is no stream of clouds being borne on the wind.

The top rocks of Gable, however, strike through the cloud, and the air up here is suddenly clearer, brighter, quieter, because it is full of sunshine from the low-hung orb. In 50 paces we pass from piercing chill to a gentle, easy atmosphere, from darkness to a radiance which can be felt. The great blue shadows of peaks and ridges are still creeping up the lower slopes ; Lingmell's sharp shoulder is seen over the white enclosures of Wasdale, nigh 2500 feet below. As we watch, other clouds seem to wander into existence ; there is one making a line above the jagged Piers Ghyll ; another in the Mosedale gap, and a great fleece which hides the Secret Valley of Buttermere.

Our mountain day is full of change : in Styhead remains a constant blot of cloud, spreading, dwindling, rising, falling, but never departing. In August it would be called the Borrowdale Sop, and a sign of bad weather, but December has its own rules; and once the sop-cloud rose so high that the sun was caught, and a halo of prismatic hues seemed to hover outside the rocks of Great End.

Southey is right when he writes of recesses discovered under snow conditions; there is a little amphitheatre among the rocks of Glaramara which has always been invisible from a distance—until today. Every rib of mountain has its sharp definition but is not stark and staring. The elements of the picture fit well: there are distant lakes, some flashing like silver swords, others mere dark shields on an expanse which is only partly snow-clad. One to the north is blue, another touched with green from the sober northern sky. Why is the sky always green over Scotland, I wonder?

Winter days are short, and soon after the sun has just peeped into the deepest glen, the shadows lengthen, blue mists appear over the lakes, and the light kindles in colour. By half past two the change is obvious: rocks which had been touched with sunshine are in shadow, and the western recesses are more than pools of gloom. Incidentally the light now touches a deep cleft in the mountains above Eskdale, which seemed to be floored with snow and guarded by mighty slabs and towers of rock. I once went to find that promising bit of work, but alas, it was an illusion! There is just a fold in a snow-seamed buttress, a place of snow-shelves, many icicles and unstable rocks.

Day's end from Great Gable is glorious: standing by the cairn there is a fine view as the sun drops into a purple dust-bank on the horizon; there is just a flicker, a path of red across the sea beyond Seascale, and then the orb fades and is hidden. But not the glory and mystery of light and colour. A rosy glow among the hills seems to be ethereal, without source, but it is merely the vivid western light swinging high into the heavens and then reflecting on the snow. But this does not seem to explain the mystery of wandering lights in the coves of other hills—blue glowing mists, purple-red folds over the Armboth moors with white Helvellyn behind, the silver of distant hills. In deep glens such as Borrowdale, Nature seems to have spilled an artist's palate of the most delicate tints—lilac, grey-blue, bronze, deep, quiet gold, with green and pale brown-red of fir and larch woods. I wonder if the folk of Borrowdale ever see such visions in their winter sunsets, or do they always look upwards to the rosy afterglow which is flooding ridge and mountain-top.

The last light suddenly fails; the sky turns pale grey-blue in the east, foreshadowing the rising arch of blue-black, even purple, darkness, spangled with planets and stars. The snow is again crisp ivory, with here and there an upturned peak touched with silver. At night Styhead pass has its own sounds—the gurgle of streamlets near and far, the soughing of the night breeze, the plash and sob of waves on the shingle round its mountain tarn. Our footsteps of morning are easily traced and serve as a guide down the roughish corridor. A sudden vision holds us at the mountain edge where Seathwaite Farm, in its tiny recess, comes into view. From the hollow is rising a silver veil—it is too frail to name as cloud—and as it passes us on its wavering course there is a distortion and every ridge and cove seems to swim in a faint silver light.

Cold Dunmail

Fair weather, like peaceful years, leaves but few memories. My recollections of Dunmail Raise, which was the last horsed-coach route in Britain, are emphasized by darkness, mist and tempest. I have crossed the great pass between Seat Sandal and Steel Fell, from Keswick to Grasmere in a midnight blackness that could be felt; I have used the route in rain that struck solid blows like the waves of a tide; I have weathered it in a blighting gale which roared through clear moonlight.

That was the starkest, coldest experience of my roadward life. The fells were ivory-white with snow, the sky was purple blue; the stars came out like great lumps of coloured gems. Yet the blast howled and crashed and froze until movement became almost impossible. Far in front was a dark patch of the lake at Grasmere with shadow on the slopes beyond. The whole was the fiercest outlook I have ever seen, or wish to see. I felt far more exhausted after that battle with an impalpable foe than when I pushed through snow-drifts a yard deep, with a blizzard hiding even the track, and every landmark smothered in white. At such a time there can be real peril for the wanderer on Dunmail Raise; the hill-side is broken into deep gullies, and the water-course is large and snow-masked.

Coming from northward, on an ordinary day, the pass is easy. The new road sweeps easily from Wythburn to the shoulder of the pass. The old winding route of my boyhood is forgotten, and grass grows on some abandoned stretches. There was a picturesque little nook where the stream broke through some ledges beneath a bunch of Scots firs, which is now only seen by the shepherd when he gathers his stock of sheep from Seat Sandal. When time permits I make another call at the old corner where I took a frugal meal on the way to and from Helvellyn. It was then the only shady spot within miles, but now the trough of Thirlmere becomes darker every year with growing conifers.

Dunmail Raise has not the romance of Shap Fell, but I claim that it is a far more ancient crossing. In the ages before man, wild geese and swans came this way from the frozen north. You can still hear

them, wings sweeping and voices hissing and calling, any midnight of
late autumn or early spring when they are flighting to and from the
Arctic north.   The Romans came over the Raise, but they did not
force the barrier of Shap Fell, dodging east through the Lune trench,
past Low Borrow Bridge, and over Orton Scar to Kirkby Thore.

From the outset, the turnpike over Dunmail Raise, with its little
toll window at Town Head, was kept up by the silver of "Lakers" who
desired to drive in comfort from one beauty-spot to the next.   Business
traffic was confined to an occasional wagon of wool from the Wythburn
farms, or to the carriers' carts which brought creature comforts from
the markets at Ambleside and Kendal.   The strings of pack-ponies
between Kendal and Whitehaven travelled mostly by way of Little
Langdale and Wrynose, and not by Grasmere and Dunmail Raise.

When railways threw an iron web across England, there was left,
and remains, a gap of 21 miles between Keswick and Windermere.
For many a year, by virtue of his Post Office contract, Richard Rigg
clothed his drivers and guards in official scarlet, and fine fellows they
were.   How one remembers that clinking of chains, the tinkle of
hooves, the occasional crack of the whip, and the harsh wheel-rattle as
the mail passed over the bridge at the foot of the Raise.   It might not
carry letters, but the colour at any rate was official enough.

Yes, and I see again old Bob drawing his team together as the coach
dipped over the last rise and began the steep fall to Grasmere.   Now,
out with the yard of tin, and blow the road clear.   Uphill traffic must
give way to the cantering, galloping mail.   And Bob sat there, remote,
silent, and even defiant until the steep two miles were passed, and he
could become a human being once again.

How he would tell you that his horses were poor—"three stiff-uns
and a bolter"—but no one believed such a tale, did they ?

CHAPTER NINE

BACK O' SKIDDAW

Remembering the Schoolmaster—Hounds are Home—Wild Beast Shows
—Hedge-side Memories.

TO all but Cumbrians "Back o' Skiddaw" is a remote wilderness,
where folks are savage and roads are rough and far between.   It
approximates to the Lancashire man's Chowbent.   It was "Back o'
Skiddaw" in the old time where one man was chairman, sole member

and clerk of the parish council, and had to elect himself to the District Council. Now there are more adults to vote, and the wild parish is combined with others. Still, I dare say you can still find traces of parish notices nailed to a door facing the mountain-path. It was up in this misty area that a shepherd's meet used to be held for the exchange of stray sheep. Like the other meeting on Sticks Pass, the liquor, when needed, came up in kegs on pony-back, for no wheeled vehicle could approach the place.

They had quaint folks "Back o' Skiddaw" in John Peel's time, and before that its tracks were doubtless known to Solway smugglers and to illicit distillers of whisky. Personally I should have avoided the last job, for the smoke from the stills must have been visible on a clear day from Skiddaw itself. John Keats wrote this about the summit :

> From off old Skiddaw's top, when fog conceals
> His rugged forehead in a mantle pale,
> With an eye guess toward some pleasant vale,
> Descry a favourite hamlet fair and far.

I am not clear that Skiddaw was one of the regular beacons which alarmed Cumberland of Scottish raids. Its summit, over 3000 feet above the sea, is often capped with mist, and invisible either from the Border or from the dales. But in times of national peril, when armies in great force were assembled to cross the Border, the beacon might be manned and lit.

Of course I know that this contemptible "Back o' Skiddaw" is John Peel's country, and that John was born, hunted and died in this neighbourhood. It was in a house at Low Caldbeck that John Woodcock Graves wrote the words of the song impromptu, and sung them to his friend, adding, "By Jove, Peel ; you'll be sung when we're both run to earth." John's favourite hunting-ground lay between the suburbs of Carlisle and the tops of Blencathra and Skiddaw, and he galloped and chased over the parishes to the Solway. However, what is "Back o' Skiddaw" to one is the world to another. The Keswick men say it in contempt of the Caldbeck folk, and the Carlisle people use it about every dweller in the dales around Derwentwater, Bassenthwaite and Thirlmere. There are farms in the coves of Skiddaw Forest to which the "First Foot" of the New Year used to come late in February, but maybe in these days the parcels postman is there on New Year's Day. I recall the days when a postman's pocket could carry every letter of a dale, when the mail for certain farms was placed in hollow trees, or in holes beneath stiles. It was no new thing to find young men and women who had never handled pen or pencil since they left school, and who had forgotten their former slow accomplishment.

Among older people there were plenty "Back o' Skiddaw" who had never learnt to write at all. I have had to read a letter for one such. He called me into the parlour from the kitchen, and locked the door mysteriously.

"My nevvy wadn't like it, but I have to make sure," he muttered as he turned out a well-thumbed sheet and asked me to read. I complained that it was merely a page from some old school-book. "I mun try agen then."

The second sheet was the right one, a letter of news from a son in some big city, and I read it through. "Fred blows so when he's reading that I can't make out what he says at times. Read it agen, lad." And I did. The mug of hot tea warmed me for the long trounce over the soaking fells to Keswick, which to the old man was a strange place and "dang it, Back o' Skidda' ye kna' ".

Remembering the Schoolmaster

In my boyhood I knew a youth who in due time became a schoolmaster in John Peel's country, but in later years our meetings were seldom, and gradually I ceased to hear of him, even through third persons. The other day I dropped into his village, and inquired. The first person told me that my friend had retired "into the teens of years ago", and that his present whereabouts was known only in a general way.

"Into the teens of years" means that he had impressed village memory to some extent.

"I was one of his scholars," said my informant; "he retired under the age limit, and had been twenty-five years in the place. But though he was a grand teacher, and brought forward a lot of clever lads, he never went much among folk. I don't think he cared about markets, fairs, horses and sheep. He was always quite agreeable, of course, never had a wrong word for or by anybody, and he did a lot of quiet and responsible work for the village, before secretaries were invented.

"Still, there were times, especially in his latter years, when it seemed that he didn't want to be among folk at all. He looked after his school work, but maybe his heart failed him a bit with the other folk. I would not be surprised—they were a long way from him, and not too civilized in their tricks."

Personally, I would never attach any blame to a teacher who, after wrestling with small replicas of three Cumberland generations, did want to sit apart a bit, and talk and think of something else.

"There were times when he would drop in at the shoemaker's

shop just at closing time for a talk, and he could be real interesting if no villager came in to stop him. No doubt at all, he was a further learned man than the schoolmaster here has need to be."

I exclaimed impatiently : "That man had a brain worthy of great things. From the school where he was taught he went forward to college and seemed likely to go right ahead. It was for his own content, and maybe for his health, that he settled on the threshold of John Peel's country. In his young days he easily carried two big appointments in industrial towns, posts which open only to men of ability. But he preferred a less bustling gait, and so he moved out of the line of big jobs. Only one of his brothers and sisters lived to see thirty, and he knew that there was danger in living too strenuously and in bad air."

"He had good air up here," exclaimed the Cumbrian ; "it's about the only thing that's both really good and plentiful at the same time."

"Do you know," said I, "I have missed inquiring for him on several occasions when I passed through the village, and I am sorry for it. There was 1919, the first New Year after the First Great War, when I came through here on a walk. I had forgotten, however, that he was here, and it was a snowy and stormy day. I had to walk through to Patterdale at the head of Ullswater, and that's a fair step from Caldbeck where I had slept the previous night, coming there in wind and snow after dark. I remember that I had dinner (or lunch) at Mungrisdale, where Jim Hutchinson was stopping. The weather had even stopped the Blencathra hounds, so it must have been bad."

I looked up the open village with its green between two roads. "There's been a change here," I said ; "what is it ?"

The Cumbrian laughed. "It's not much that escapes your eyes. It's only a little tree standing where the old 'George' used to be ; you know it was empty for years and falling into ruins. The old Squire was a ter'ble teetotaller, and he bought out the 'George' and closed its license. It was never let again. The windows and doors went down and the bairns used to scramble up and down it. So the Council at last condemned it as dangerous, though, mind you, it was bad to bring down. The masons had a job. The lime-mortar, even that used for filling, had set as hard as stones, and it took a lot of labour to shift it out, bit by bit.

"The old market-house there has had its adventure as well. The building at the far side has a green-doored garage. A new driver got his car out, and instead of reversing to get clear, he put the gear into second, and crashed right up and against the pillar, crumpling up the radiator of his car and bringing down a pile of old rubbish. The man wasn't much hurt : they said he rolled out as the car hit against the pillar, and left it. The insurance men came down day after day but how it all ended I don't know. The market-house has not fallen down yet."

I reverted to our former friend, the schoolmaster. "No," said the Cumbrian, with a smile ; "he didn't put on much flesh up here. The wind is too bitter for such as him to do that. He was a quiet-living man, and managed all right. I did hear that a year or two back he had to have an operation, but so far as I know he is still alive. So far as I know, he has not come back to the old school. The bairns soon grow out of kenning, and like enough he will not have a big amount of interest in some of the thicker-headed sort of folk that have grown on to old men and women on the farms and in the cottages. He always declared that the brightest lads and lassies would never live in John Peel's country. Mighty few of them have come back once they leave, except, it may be, for a bit of a fishing holiday or something of the sort. The schoolmaster would know the place, even the school all right, but the folks have grown up."

Hounds are Home

Old Jonty of Hesketh used to revile August as, with church-warden in his claws and a beer-pot on the table, he sat at ease in the little inn. "It's the only time o' year one gits mad wi' the huntsman. What's he want wi' calling all the hounds in to Threlkel' kennels ? They want none of his physicking and training ; we keep 'em in rare fettle, and we can do wi' a bit o' hunting on Sundays. They tell me that old John Crozier, when he was a lad, blew his horn for the hounds which were living out on the farms, and in ten minutes the whole pack was on its road from even six mile away."

That's many a year since, but in our dales there is the same restive and resentful spirit at this season. It's over-keenness that does it, and the trouble soon passes when the sound of the horn is heard from the hills or across the meadows. Among the fells of Cumbria the fox-packs are broken up at the end of each season, and hounds are "walked" by various enthusiasts, some of whom think it only fair to snatch many a summer hunt against marauding foxes. In such manner the dales-men, shepherds, farmers and quarry lads teach themselves the rudi-ments of hunting over wild country, and many of them become experts in handling little groups of hounds in difficult conditions. They find too the tracks by which foxes travel across the hills, and the binks or ledges on which they lie and sleep, hidden from view among heather or bracken. This is all to the good, but there are elements which are unwelcome to the huntsman who has to show sport with the pack all winter.

All great huntsmen have their ideas about condition. The poor hounds return from "walk" bulging with evidence that the flesh-pots have been too accessible, and the week-end hunt, beloved of Jonty's type, is a mere scamper compared with the hard gruelling of the four-or-five-days-a-week season. I heard one old huntsman grumble: "The young missus, she's from the south I think, said to me, quite bright, 'I've seen that the hound has taken no harm.' I said, 'Thank ye.' But I near on said overmuch when summat about as big as a cauf came waddling round the corner, and near on knocked me down. It was old Ruby, and what a mess the poor beggar was in." Kindness in food becomes a refined cruelty to a fox-hound sometimes.

During the first week or so at kennels a strict diet corrects most of the bulges of flesh, and "pack psychology" or the hunting spirit gradually controls the hounds' behaviour. During summer they have run wild, and all are in savage high spirits. The whip is not a kennel implement in Cumbria, but the huntsman's orders must be smartly obeyed—and the hounds know it. There are scamps which will truant to the village and feed heavily, and often thievishly; there are some which have not found competitors to meet their scrapping and wrestling strength. The wise huntsman allows a certain amount of liberty in these matters, but long ere the "opening day" he will have the whole pack "at a word", and woe betide the blunderer, the wayward, the stubborn or heedless one. The next few weeks are anxious and arduous ones for the mountain huntsman; he must test his hounds, provide them with walking exercise, and bring the pack to the finely-tempered hunting-tool it was last spring. Will old Bountiful be able to gallop again? Is Crafty's rheumatism more serious? Which of the young draft will be able to run beside this or that veteran, and learn from it all the niceties of the chase? After all, Jonty's type of man may grumble, but while he is idle from his fox-chases, the huntsman is having no easy time at kennels; there is much essential work to be packed into the coming weeks if hunting is to go on through the winter without a break.

Wild Beast Shows

As the fatted animals gradually move out of our Lake Country farms to the winter markets, new cattle must come in, and the services of the "beas' jobber" are often in keen demand. He lives arduous days and nights, galloping, or roaring in his car, here and there, picking up stirks in high-lying parishes, attending remote auction marts and even farm sales. Most of the traders have regular sources of supply, but occasionally these fail, or the demand is unusually high.

Then the more active member of the firm gets the order for close search. "Gan thee up to Troutbeck, an' see Willie Clerk o' Mell Fell End; he's like to ha' some o' t' reet soo-art; and it's a good township for beas'."

This Troutbeck, between Keswick and Penrith, is really a wild high moor, quite unlike its name, with one lonesome inn, and the young jobber steps off the train into a yard of snow. "Nay, there's nae motor-car, lad, for them lanes; what, even a trap couldn't git through the drifts, and our horse isn't well, anyway, and couldn't be ventured. Isaac, thee show t' young chap t'rooad to Willie Clerk's; it's nut so far."

Isaac the aged hobbles up the broken track in the snow to the top of the long hill, then points. "There's Willie's; but there's a goodish bit o' sna." Over the deceptive white, End Farm seems a short mile away, but there is tribulation on the route. Let the young jobber tell his story, as he sits back after a hard day of trade.

"Why, man, in five minutes after Isaac went I was hid in a deep trough, and there was a hundred or two waves all drifted deep, and then, at a strong beck, I missed the foot-plank, and tramped an hour afore I could cross—and Willie Clerk's wasn't a foot nearer at the end.

"However, in three hours I crept up to Willie's, tired as a dog already, and telt him I wanted to buy. 'Hev a cup o' tay,' says he, 'rum was finished at Christmas.' Then he mustered oot what stirks he hed—they were poor, and of course I spak oot. 'Nay, nay, them's nea use to me; I mun git 'em better—ha' ye better stuff?' Willie was a bit huffed. 'Weel noo, lad, thee tak' ma advice: thou may know what thou wants, but nivver tell a farmer that his stirks are no good; he'll mek thee pay for it sometime.'

"However, Willie held no grudge; he showed me a fine heifer, and what, man, I just hed to buy it—at his price, but it was a gradely good deal for me. Then Willie, he said: 'I'll lend thee a pony and a lad; he'll tak' thee to Mr. Nelson's, and mappen thou'll hear there summat o' what thou wants. T'lad 'll bring t' pony back all right; he knows where the drifts and fords are.'"

So the day passed; Nelson had a few of the right sort; so had his neighbour Crosthwaite, and so had Chapman. The young jobber began to see his consignment filled up. Then Nelson said: "By gum, lad, but thou's benighted; I wod offer thee a bed but the missis is bad. Let's gan on to the pub at Mungrisdale; mappen they'll put thee up."

"Yes," continued the jobber, "but it wasn't an easy job; t'auld lad wasn't varra willing, neither was t' missus, and Nelson had to persuade 'em. And every now and again somebody ud peep round the lang settle at me, and then they would argue again. At last Nelson come back to me. 'I've made it all right for thee ; good night.' They gave me a poor supper, and a bed that, thinly clothed that I was, near starved, forbye the window was loose in its frame and jaddered a'most as much as my teeth. I didn't sleep much ; breakfast wasn't owt grand. When it come to paying up, I said to landlord, "What's up as ye're all so shy and rough to me ?" 'Well now,' he said, as he picked up my shillings, 'we thowt as mappen thou was ane o' them embezzling clerks as we read sae mitch about, wi' they fine town ways and talk.' Hum! I don't fancy that any embezzler would lodge in Mungrisdale for a day—they're that curious folk."

Next morning, still over snow-covered parishes, the search for good beasts continued, and then at Hesketh Newmarket there is chance to hire a pony. At one farm the trade takes time. The old chap had married a widow with several sons, and they all had a hand in the trade. It was funny ; the jobber on his pony outside the house ; the old man asking pleadingly, "Won't you gi' a bit more ?" "No." He runs back to the porch where the family is hidden, and comes back with another argument or assurance. The jobber tumbles to the game, and makes up his mind to a price, and finally, after an extra long conference in the porch, "We think ye'll ha' to have 'em, but—it's a poor price." At another farm a fine heifer was seen, and a bargain was struck with the farmer, old Job Price. And so back to the old inn at lonely Troutbeck.

"Well, lad, I thowt we'd lost ye, but Isaac saw ye crossing to Edward Nelson's on the pony, and so-a we knew that there was a lang journa' for ye. How have ye come on ?

"And ye bought Job Price's heifer. Well, well—but Mary'll ha' something to say about that."

A few days later there was a "tryst" at the inn to which the cattle from different farms were driven, and the jobber took delivery, giving payment on the spot.

"All there—aye, all but Job Price's heifer."

"Aye, aye ; I said Mary ud ha' summat to say about that."

"Well, I'm goin' to git it."

"Thou'll nut."

"Lend's the pony, and I'll fetch it in."

"Tell thee what, thou s'all ha' the pony for nowt if thou does."

"Aye, and I'll pay double for it if I don't."

"Aye," said the cattle-dealer, ruminatively, "she was right after all. I trotted the pony across to the Price farm, but long afore I come near I catches sight of old Job toddling off up the ghyll and away to the fell. He was miles in front of me. I went to the farm, tried the kitchen door, went across to the shippon and stable: all locked up and as quiet as death.   Then I went and tried the door again.   A woman's head peered out of an upstairs window; sour as crab verjuice she looked and talked.

" 'What's tha want, rattling and knockin' theer ?'

" 'I want t'heifer I bowt t'other day.'

" 'Thou's nut gaen to git her,' she rasped, and slammed the window. And I had to pay double for the pony.

"Up round Blencathra way there's nut many like Mary Price, and everybody soon kens 'em—except strangers."

Hedge-side Memories

In our remote Lakeland dale the schoolmaster used to be parish clerk and general surveyor if the priest were a student or muddler and not a semi-farmer with fields to plough and mow.   In my young days, much work was still done by labouring contractors—thrashing, draining, hedging, peat-cutting, walling, mowing, and even catching moles at a farthing an acre.   Every juvenile farmer was expected to "figure a bit" in order to check accounts or make estimates.

In the dear old hedge-side school, teams of older lads were regularly turned out to measure and value estate jobs, and the calculations had to bear both practical and theoretical tests.   Four of us, with a string knotted in feet, a slate and pencil, would ramble off to a stack-yard and take the girth, height, etc., of a cylinder of straw, topped with a cone.   Old Tom Preston would jeer at our effort, "No farmer wants to measure straw."   The stonebreaker at the cross-roads peevishly hindered our efforts, for he alleged that our novice bunglings caused his neat oblongs to slide out of shape.   "Ye're never right either; the schooly's figures are always less than mine."

Jimmy, the fierce old chap with a face red as the harvest moon, wanted an estimate of hours to be spent in threshing, but we were only concerned in reckoning the number of bags of seed to be produced.

"Shaff on ye," he said ; "you can't figure except when schooly does it for you."

However, we sat down beyond the next hedge and pencilled out the new sum—the result of which a daring one shouted across the field to the farmer.

Reckoning up fence walling and draining was easy enough, but sometimes a factor would be ignored, and the village inn rang with laughter.   "Them lads as was out measuring reckoned as I sud ha'e forty pound for building that bit of wall.   They wad pay me for every square foot instead of the price a foot run." However, some of our teams earned renown. The squire asked once the name of a lad who had measured up a great mass of quarried rock, and had done it correctly. But he roared at the next calculation by which the same lad brought the timber in the park to small stick indeed.

Country measurements were difficult: the ordinary cubic and square scales were almost unknown, and one worked by the rood (which was a pole or rod), by the fall (about 22 square yards), by the square in thatching, and by quite different and arbitrary rules for everything else. There was a conspiracy not to divulge these terms to the lads at school lest they should be as wise as their elders.

By mistakes and disappointments the team learnt something of Practice with Science in farm surveying, at any rate, but it was a harsh school, and sometimes one had to bite a lip lest it should tremble, wink the eyes lest tears should fall. Our errors always leaked out to the farmers and were exaggerated when they met us in the lanes and public places, but, on the other hand, it was a great delight when some ancient worker asked us to practise on his finished but unpaid-for job. Lofty had "eyed" the task and quoted a lump sum for it, but the new agent decided a contract at so much a square yard. The old man was "no scholard" and feared that he would be a loser. He was—to the extent, we told him, of 5d. on his ten pounds and a crown. And the agent's measuring-line confirmed our knotted string absolutely. Next time we emerged from the school to measure a field we had more confidence, but oh, the weary hours of calculation we had in store. The job had to be finished ere we were allowed to go home.

CHAPTER TEN

POACHER YARNS

Poacher's Night—Poacher Lass—Smiddy John—Jimmy Green, Wise Man

IT is unfashionable to write about the erring folk of our country-side except from the lofty standpoint either of the magistrate who is interested in their punishment or the missioner who spends a good deal of useable time in reforming them. I'm not interested in either. There is a family in our village which is a notoriously bad lot. For generations their feuds have kept the police busy, and their depredations are always landing one or other in gaol. They have some pride in a longer descent than any of the villagers who cannot tell where Grandfather or Grandmother was born. In the kitchen of the awful family one has heard stories of old-time adventures in gaol.

There was Grand-uncle Basty who was so often in gaol that they made him waiter for the warders' dinner. One day he was standing at the table in the open hall, when he heard a familiar whistle. Without turning round, he indicated that he "knew". Whereupon from the cell above came the words of Grand-uncle Gallus, "I'se clemmed; chuck's a bite." Basty's privilege included the finishing of any surplus food on the warders' table, and he had a goodly chunk of pie-crust in his hand. In a moment the food had been jerked backward over his shoulder, and Gallus made sure of it. The chief warder, however, saw the action and poor Basty got the reward of three months in gaol with the loss of all privileges.

Uncle Lant of the family had a fine voice, and a love for the Governor of the grey stone gaol. Nothing pleased Lant better than to practise and sing an ant'em on Christmas morning in the grim chapel. He is reported to have said to a magistrate who would have acquitted him for some November theft: "But, Mr. Fletcher, can't you send me to gaol? It's getting near Christmas, and a month is a short time for me to get up a new ant'em."

"How did Basty get that name?"

"I don't know; his mother always said that it was a nasty nickname —same as Gallus—and if any man ever did deserve to hang on a gallows it was that one." Of course Basty is short for Bastille: some of our old prisons held the name of the famous (or infamous) French fortress until about half a century ago. This can be proved from old letters and records of country conversations.

The rogue family believe that the following yarn belongs to Grand-uncle Gallus. He had been taken red-handed in theft, and haled before the judge. He pleaded guilty; the case seemed clear; and His Honour merely indicated that the jury must convict and that sentence to death for sheep-stealing would follow. In a short time, however, the jury returned a verdict of "Not Guilty", and the judge stormed. The foreman merely looked as knowing as he could, and then answered here: "That's all right, but you see, Mr. Judge, we know Gallus better than you do: if he pleads guilty to this, we know that he's doing it to hide something far worse."

Violence runs in such families: one of them was cutting peat on the moor when a keeper whom he hated came into sight. The scoundrel gave up working, stalked his victim, and when the man was crossing a wet bog he was attacked and cut down with the sharp-edged spade (a fearful weapon). Luckily two other keepers saw the attack and ran

"HOUNDS COME HOME": ESKDALE AND ENNERDALE PACK IN LITTLE LANGDALE

LITTLE GREY SHEEP. ROUND UP OF HERDWICKS ON SNOW-COVERED DUNMAIL RAISE, WITH HELM across. They found the poacher coolly standing on the breast of the unconscious man, and forcing the face deeper into the ooze and water. There was a desperate battle ere the victim was rescued. Before the judge the poacher was hard as stone : he remarked to the witness who still showed signs of damage, "Aye, and if them other fellows hedn't come up, it's a ghost thou'd be this instant minute."

These "bad lots" made fierce wars among themselves on little provocation; and their women were often in the front of the affray. Two old rogues lived in a shed on the moor ; one had a dog, the other a cat. "Ben, thou likes thy dog," sneered one. The other retorted, "And thou likes thy cat." So they fell to blows—one using a short scythe-blade which had been kept for bracken-cutting, the other a heavy bar from a smithy. All day they fought, and in the end both were so badly knocked about that a doctor had to be brought. There was evidence enough of insanity to send both to the lunatic asylum—but the tribe always believed that they were not madder than their average.

The doctor was the only Christian at one time who dare answer a call from these wild rebels against law and decency. He usually came through all right, unless the rival sept threw bricks as he left the house of sickness and death. Unless armed with a warrant, the constable of the old type had to leave the settlement alone or suffer grievously. The womenfolk were a disgrace to their sex—and gloried in it. A good religious woman who felt a call to help them came out of the hovels with her face streaming with blood and her clothes rent to rags. She declined to prosecute, and the tribe's gratitude for many a year was shown by lavishing on her the best spoils of salmon river, grouse moor, or pheasant copse.

One's personal dealings with the tribe were a bit guarded : to associate openly with them meant the loss of one's good character. "A man is known by the company he keeps", however, isn't an infallible maxim by any means. Sometimes a sample of such company is sufficient to give one a broader outlook on life. It takes all sorts to make a world, they say; but the Basty-Gallus lot have had to be fumigated out of it. A man's memories would be dull indeed if he only saw one class. That's why the autobiographies of the very good are so rarely read. The weak and rough and rebellious have always mildly interested me—I wonder why? Certainly I've never been tempted to take up a crusade on their behalf.

Poacher's Night

Our bridge-end poacher is a stern individualist. He sees no mortal sin in his raids on fin, fur and feather, but he would vigorously protect

I

such property from vulgar hands. The puerile idea of a magistrate that owners of fisheries should share their facilities with the unemployed rouses much ire in his heart. A communism of natural resources is anathema. In five years the estuary nets would wipe out the last remaining salmon ; in a week the villagers would destroy all the trout. "For a wee bit of time there'd be rare doin's, and then there'd be nowt for ivver."

The salmon is a rover, and the poacher must take him as he can. The trout, however, moves but little in favourable waters. A few miles upstream to the spawning-ground in late autumn and a sad, tired return after the duties of family life mark the usual boundaries of excursions, though now and again river trout, their scales silvered in the salt, are taken in estuary and deep-water nets.

Throughout the year the trout is exposed to its many enemies. Kelly alleges that disappointed Waltonians will sweep up a big fish in their landing-nets or trap it in a noose of gut worked from the rod-point. He has seen a learned professor prone on the wet bank guddling for the tiny trout which persistently took refuge under the swinging grass fringe. He even accuses others of raking the pools with a long line stretched from bank to bank.

"If they knew how we worked the otter in the old days, they would use that as well." The floating board, leaded on its keel to catch the breeze, was used to carry the baited lines over the promising waters beyond reach of the angler's cast. The result was that many trout were pricked by nibbling at the baits without being actually brought ashore. A pricked fish, like the burnt child, shuns any moving bait, whether fly, minnow, or worm.

The above processes, Kelly complains, are of little use to the professional, who must get many fish in order to pay his way. They are merely illegal practices without the saving grace of wholesale application. Poached trout are not passed at normal prices. Kelly has to be content with the work of capture, the risk of detection, for about one-sixth of the market value. No decent poacher will resort to the guddling or poisoning of fish with chloride and other deleterious chemicals. Nor will he "shoot" the water with a stick of gelignite or a Mills bomb. A hundred trout may be destroyed by such methods to every dozen picked up, and the pool will be swept clear of the small fry which afford food for bigger fish for a considerable time to come.

The sweep of the net remains the popular manner of taking large quantities of trout. Poaching on a large scale needs a gang. One man on either bank draws the net rope forward, the third and maybe others wade behind and clear the net from rocks and other obstructions.

The work has to be done in darkness, and furtively, for the police are
as alert nowadays as the bailiffs and keepers.

But, says Kelly, it isn't the poaching itself that's difficult.   To carry
a fine net down to a well-watched stream and to get the gang together
is a bit hard, but to get the fish away is the very devil.   It's particularly
hard in places where every cart or trap is well-known, and even a
motor-car can be made to stand and deliver if suspected of trout-
carrying.   The motor-lorries would be all right if one could be sure
that the drivers would not sell on e to the police, and that the fish would
get to their right place at the end·   Dave Dodgeon gave a rare haul to
the chap driving EU960, but he never heard anything more of them.

Somehow the local drivers aren't just the right sort to trust : they
depend too much on the police looking soft about licences and speeds
to do any side job which might bring them before the bench.   Besides,
they are always fined with the gang, where in the old time the donkey-
cart hawker was let off with a warning.

Poacher Lass

The country-side hates poacher lasses.   Blowsy, impudent, with
shrieking invective for the slightest imagined occasion, long of vicious
memories, they pretend to peddle small wares, gather nuts, mushrooms
or blackberries.   "Aye, there's Sal Robson on her round again," says
the keeper.   "I'll have to go down and pick up any snares she has laid."
The woman poacher fears nothing : she will lay snares in broad daylight, and trespass into the most sacred coverts with nonchalance.
"Not only that," complains John, "but she'll pick up a net lost last
night and swear that it has tumbled from her basket.   No, she's never
prosecuted, though she's at the back of most game trouble in this
neighbourhood."

In one village there are three generations of poacher lasses, but
their snares and nets were confined to hares and rabbits, plunderers of a
bit of garden next the park.   A certain honour influenced them, for
every spring a hen pheasant nested untouched in their plot, and a covey
of partridge always sheltered in their garden dyke.   Another old lady
decreed death for any salmon she could spear, but her girls were
"respec'able, aye, every one of 'em", she used to chuckle.   "They
wouldn't even use a garden fork when dinner for a week was splashing
and rattling about in the shallow dub next the house."

Sal Robson is perhaps an exception ; she comes, as we say, of a bad
lot : poachers, drinkers, thieves, every one of them.   Sal is keen at
marketing her game ; as she becomes stouter and less active she will

undoubtedly leave the outdoor work to her menfolk and act as selling-agent. Already her fraternity have marked her power, and old John knows that dozens of hares and pheasants are passing through her hands. Poacher Sal isn't easily caught. A search-warrant has been tried in vain. John believes that the haul of game was hidden beneath some floor. "My dog was right uneasy, so I'm sure the birds were somewhere near, but the police wouldn't stop any longer. I never heard such swearing as Sal and her cousins used. Next time I'll put a bit of wax in my ears, and tell the sergeant to do the same."

Sal was brought up to be a poacher. Even when she was a wee nipper she would slip out into the fields and make daisy chains while the old lurcher raced after a hare or rabbit. She was bold as brass at bringing in the game. At present she is rather tolerated—police and keepers have no desire to place her in the dock if they can check her tricks on game. However, the inevitable will happen one of these days—probably through her selling activity, which will bring raiders from another district. Then Sal will have to use more than bad language to escape punishment.

Smiddy John

Poacher tools are increasingly hard to obtain since the blacksmith gave way to the motor-fitter in our villages. We used to look innocent when Smiddy John beat out and barbed a thin sliver of steel. With two other prongs it was welded to a frame, and became a formidable fish-spear. If you wanted to buy such a weapon, you chaffered with John for pigs, and went out to the sty to choose a porker that didn't grunt. The fish-spear was always hidden beneath the thatch; there may be one hidden there and forgotten today.

"There's a lot of fish up; I've sold five pigs," said Smiddy John contemplatively. "I shouldn't wonder if somebody wanted a sixth tonight."

Smiddy would also curve a bit of tinplate round a farmer's lantern, and turn the honest round beacon into a furtive wee lamp which would throw narrow beams into the deep pools. The salmon sailed lazily to the surface, within the reach of the waiting spear, and would be struck.

"Yet," said Smiddy John, "my father sold spears by the dozen—and there was fish in every pool in his time." Since Smiddy John's time the salmon are scarcer still, it hardly pays to poach them.

A century ago salmon-spearing was a royal sport. At Balmoral gillies and guests alike turned out to strike fish, and Queen Victoria rejoiced in the picturesque tumult. Everyone was drenching wet in no time, and Her Majesty's diary shows with glee that one important personage measured his length in a deep place, overbalanced by making a stroke at a big fish, and had to be rescued.

I have seen old fish-spears in many a Border village, and at clachans near Highland streams they were fairly common. The gillies were not above "driving the water", after the last guest had departed for the south, and the fish remained in good condition. I am told that in remote Western Ireland today, salmon are still speared in the old way, and even go to market with great lance-strokes through sides and shoulders.

Smiddy John always had wires for snares, had genius to repair the two-piece gun which had been damaged during a raid after pheasants, and he stocked rings and other tackle in a score convenient forms. But John never tried the temper of his wares—and he demanded cash down. "Yes, pay me in pheasants—and get me into your bother? Not for John, it's cash or no trade. Beside, I never knew a man who mended himself of being hard up by poaching. A conny lot has lost brass they still have to earn by trying it on."

John himself cared little for night craft; it's wet and cold and dowly—and the odds are that you're caught once in seven times. It pays better to make tools for other folks.

Jimmy Green, Wise Man

Are there any "far-learned" chaps in our villages today? Time was when the ownership of a few tattered books and a mysterious demeanour gave the reputation. The wise man never read his library when common folk were astir: I much doubt if Jimmy Green ever opened a page at any time of his later life. His poor brain, bemused and befogged, couldn't read even a newspaper.

For all his solemn drivel, Jimmy, of Kent Dale, was a fraud. His books were without labels, and I always wanted to open and read them. Indeed, my good grandmother was afraid that I should succeed, and be turned into a pillar of salt or be consumed by fire. There were strange lights in the Wise Man's cottage when the master was from home—and some called it the Devil, but others just Jimmy's friends, the fish-poachers.

Jimmy looked wisest, they told me, when his skin was full of ale. He was stupidly vacant at most other times, though he babbled about wonderful mathematical secrets he had solved in his own mind. He could "square the circle" with one row of figures, "make the clock strike less than one", and even decided "who was Cain's wife". But the secrets died with him.

Jimmy, who was very old and shaky when I knew him, had a horror of "half-eddicated lads as set theirsel's up to kna' summat". He teased the vicar (or said he did) with abstruse and unanswerable propositions. "Nay, Jimmy; I'm college-bred, but you know the better answer", was said to be the parson's reply. But the housekeeper asserted that Jimmy's visit was not to propound new scientific discoveries but to get a pair of the vicar's old trousers. "Him and me, ye kna, are varra like in size and in hee-ad-pieces too—and what for sudn't I fill his breeches for him when they're old ones? It's cheaper than buying new."

Jimmy was a wreck; much of his mysterious talk was doubtless due to derangement. He had the renown of a good joker, but failed to raise any more laughter. He sighed, looked wise, and I suppose imbibed more free beer than any other man in the town. One cure he performed. A poor donkey was marooned on an island on which the flood was fast encroaching, but it would not face the wooden bridge which led to safety. Many tried to bring it over, and got bites or kicks for their pains. Jimmy shambled up, solemnly turned the donkey round and backed it across rumbling timber and racing water, a triumph he never forgot. "What else wad ha'e saeved the innocent donkey?" he would ask.

A generation before he had led the lads to the grammar school to demand a holiday to go nutting. He then wore a more or less academical gown and hat, and terrified the little old schoolmaster by bouncing through the window instead of the door, and screaming in three languages, Latin, Greek and Hebrew. He got them the half-day.

Even in his dotage Jimmy had a few tags of Latin, but none of us students could get him to show them off. I am told that Jimmy's "wisdom" came through over-study when he was young. He was weak, and forced his brain to a course of work until it partially gave way. His parents left him a small and carefully guarded freehold, and for half a century he lived on its income. It provided him with shelter, bread-and-cheese, and a little beer. Jimmy begged a bit to save charges for clothes, and made the little beer go a long way by apeing great learning, and accepting pints and quarts because he was "sic a clever chap, and far-larn't no end",

Chapter Eleven

LITTLE GREY SHEEP OF THE FELLS

THE land of the Herdwick sheep, the little grey monarch of the fells, extends in a crescent from St. Bees Head on the Irish Sea to the backbone of England at Stainmore Forest. For the most part it is wild, tumbled territory, rising up again and again to the 3000-feet contour. In autumn the sheep are withdrawn from the highest and most exposed walks, and winter round the daleshead farms, where the pastures are carefully preserved for their use.

Herdwick sheep range over miles of unfenced country, but they have a homing tendency which prevents voluntary wandering. A sheep must be driven from the place where it was bred with its mother ewe by a bad-tempered neighbour before it will move. After lambing-time in early May the flock will be driven back to the high fells where the grass will be growing, and will scatter to its usual haunts. A pair of sheep here come cropping among apparently dead grass tufts outside my tent-door, and something akin for love to them surges up within me. Many fore-elders of mine worked among these mountain sheep, and lived and died in lonely cottages, most of which are now in ruins. Circumstances decided that I should go elsewhere for a living, but I come back when I can to look on the sheep and to witness the craft of the mountain shepherd.

Every census shows that there are fewer real shepherds among the fells. Every smit-book, too, shows that great farms are now ranching out the little ones, and Herdwick stocks are always being reduced in number.

The mountain folk are now looking forward to lambing-time; the breeding ewes have been brought near the farms, and get a little hay on wet and stormy days. The turnip is a costly relish only given to the sickly. The weather is now of supreme importance; a harsh drought cripples the young lambs and their mothers cannot give them full milk in gale and clashy weather, and pneumonia in some form or other is fatal to new-born lambs. The Herdwick ewe is usually a good mother to her one lamb, twins being an exception among these sheep.

The quiet old dogs are now used when the flock must be driven, and the pace is kept steady indeed. Over-driven ewes bring forth dead or weak progeny. With lambing-time the shepherd has long hours and hard labour. He must see that every ewe and its lamb are reconciled. Some of the young mothers start away from the bleating, unsteady creature which would draw at their milk, and the shepherd must see that nature is duly satisfied.　After the lamb's first drink the ewe snuffs it over, and only a foolish dog would then threaten to part them.　A charging sheep is rather a formidable enemy.

I always look forward to the day in May when the shepherd takes out again the long stick with the crook at end, which is a great help in gathering a startled ewe or in turning a lamb towards its captured mother.　In this Herdwick country the crooks are cut from rowan, ash or hazel, with the proper natural shape.　Elsewhere the crook is of metal, and there is a definite curve which the smith must obtain in addition to a smooth finish, so that ewe or lamb are never caught by the wool or throttled.

Tradition says that the Herdwick, the little grey sheep of the fells, is descended from a tiny flock which came ashore from a vessel of the Spanish Armada, wrecked somewhere near Ravenglass.　Though so hardy and suited to the wild country, there is no doubt of their comparatively late origin, for records of old times show that the mountain sheep were primitive and poor-looking creatures.　The Herdwick is small of size ; it is active as a goat, but it is a tidy and well-looking type of sheep.

In the days when diners liked their mutton old and full of rich juices, the Herdwick was more in favour with gourmets.　Nowadays the taste is all for flaccid and watery "lamb", immature flesh, say the northern flock-masters, in disgust.　There is a tang about mutton which has fed on mountain herbs which is far different to anything nurtured on roots and artificial diet in south country fields.　The Herdwick should be king of sheep for the table.

"While Shepherds Watch"

The last squall of the Christmas Eve storm drummed past the old sheep-farm just after the bearded old flock-master finished reading his favourite chapter—the story of the Shepherds abiding in the fields outside Bethlehem in old Judea.　He looked up inquiringly in the sudden silence, and the shepherd lad at the foot of the table stepped across the flagged floor and opened the door.

"Nae maer wind," he reported ; "but t'sna's fa'ing thick.　I can see nowt."

As the wind fell, the air cleared.　Report after report came from the door, and soon all the men were out of their chairs, clattering on the stones, winding great scarves or shawls round their necks, donning oil-skins and thigh-boots. "They stops the snow and cold," was said. They are the complete winter gear of the sheepwalks.

I pleaded to join the work, but the sturdy old man in his arm-chair refused, while the shepherds who had the most difficult ground went off. "It's starving work and very trying." But later he permitted me to take part in a nearer patrol, and the experience was great. When we stepped out, the storm had been forgotten; the moon was riding fairly low in a sky sprinkled with stars. All round us the mighty Westmorland fells shouldered up, bearing mantles of white and with never a cloud on their heads and sides.

"It will be grander still after the moon's gone down," said the youngster at my side as I caught breath in surprise at the glory and majesty around us. "Aye," he continued sagely, "and the wind may rise again at daylight, and there'll be some drifting with this dry snow. Man, it travels in clouds and buries everything. Often the kitchen lamp never goes out for a week because all the windows are drifted up with thirty foot of snow."

Though all the sheep had been brought down from the high moun-tain pastures in early November, there is danger in a Christmas storm. The breeding flock round the farm itself may be buried in snow ("overblown") as they shelter among the rocky tors and in deep folds and cliffs on the nearer pasture. Some of these home enclosures extend over hundreds of acres of rifted and broken land, and in the coves the sheep select their winter quarters soon after their arrival. In open weather their choice has sufficient grass, but snow makes them depend on the ration of hay brought by the sledge where the going is practicable or on the shoulders of the attendant shepherd. At other times the shepherd may have to break a trail through the snow for his flock, even a couple of miles in length.

This December gale had lasted three whole days, during which very few sheep would feed. It was, therefore, necessary to drive some, from exposed parts of the pasture, to the farm. As we left the kitchen the flock-master, whose rheumatism would not allow him to travel out-doors in stormy weather, warned me.

"Go slow; Willie's a bit strong o' the leg, but keep him back. There's many a hidden rock over which both of you can trip and be lost in deep snow."

The frosty air cut like a knife; my throat and eyes ached for a few seconds until the blood was driven back to its place. "We don't need dogs on these night jobs," said the youth as we passed the outhouse which serves as kennels for the collies. "It's too cold for them, and they can't run or scent as they do by daylight. But, never fear, their job will come tomorrow, Christmas Day, as it will be, if the wind rises and there is any drifting." As we walked along, he pointed out a steep rocky place which last winter was overblown for weeks. The sheep in its shelter was located by the collies, and dug out after a fortnight's exposure to hunger, cold and darkness.

In his rapid Westmorland dialect the youth proceeded to demolish the cold theory. "It's warm inside the snow ; anyway, every sheep was in a little hole or cave of its own for the snow melted or shrunk away from their fleeces. I went into one of these holes, and it was warm enough to choke you." Willie had overlooked the natural heat of the sheep, which is conserved by the drift, also the woolly reek, so familiar to him, which would have choked me. A sheep can breathe through an ordinary snowdrift where a man would perish for lack of oxygen. Therefore a week or so in the grip of the snow is a mere incident in the life of a fell sheep. It is only when rain falls and is followed by frost, forming an ice-plate over the snow, that the flock-master becomes really worried, to summon the best "markers" among the collies, and to prepare for night and day work with spades among the snow. After this Christmas Eve storm of ours, the immediate job was to bring to shelter any and every sheep which was on its feet or lying in dangerous places.

My attention was split between the lore of the shepherd and the impressive, even oppressive, majesty of our surroundings. I could see great cliffs on the familiar peaks all draped in white ; here and there was the flash of tumbling waters, and as Willie and I came round a sharp slope we saw beneath us the silver shield of a mountain tarn all lit up by the moon's beams.

Again my breath was caught by the sheer beauty, stark, cold and even menacing though it was, of the scene. Willie was less impressionable.

Can you hear the village band ? It must be playing at the Hall two mile from here and the carols are quite distinct. It must be about eleven o'clock ; when it nears twelve, they get towards the church so that the bandsmen as are bell-ringers can help to ring the peal on Christmas midnight.

Eleven o'clock on a white Christmas Eve, and at work protecting a flock like the shepherds of old Bethlehem—the memory was startling. Under the guidance of Willie I had left the farm at nine, and for two hours our movements had been directed, not to guard the flock from bears and lions, but to drive them into safe positions against the onslaught of a gale. The sheep had been Willie's care : I had driven in this grumbling ewe, and that as he directed, but the response had been mechanical for my brain was impressed by vast peaks, white moors, the silver shield of the tarn, the brilliant moonlight, and the soft radiance of the highest stars.

"Will we be out here at midnight ?" I asked Willie, and great was my delight when he replied, "Yes, if we do our job thorough." He had accepted me as partner before this—when I let down the bars into a wood, and drove some stupid sheep into its shelter.

I think that Willie wanted to hear the midnight bells just as much as I did, so we examined every shadow, hollow and rock critically. Suddenly (abruptly, it seemed to us), the moon dropped below the horizon and her puzzling silver light was no more. Instead, the stars leapt up into steady glory : "It's thinner in the shadow when the moon's gone, and easier to work. I wouldn't have sent out the shepherds till after moon-setting, but the master's always for early hours," said the youth.

As the minutes sped, there seemed to be an increasing silence. Music no longer came from the Hall ; a light here and there on the road showed that travellers were afoot. Silently we gathered more and more sheep ; here and there a party trotted up without being sought for, and as the church clock tolled the hour of twelve we stopped at the top of a long rise. "While shepherds watched !" I rejoiced to myself as I looked across the small mob of steaming woollies in our charges. "Merry Christmas", shouted Willie from the other wing of the flock. And at that the joy-bells of the dale began to ring. Another Christmas had come to the wilderness where shepherds were guarding their flocks against storm.

Soon after midnight we two returned to the farm kitchen, and had the season's welcome. Then the head shepherd went out to the door where the weather-glass was hung, and struck a match. "We've done well to move those sheep tonight ; the glass is dropping fast." And Christmas dawn brought the roughest gale the farm had known for years.

THE END

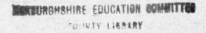

INDEX